Critical Praise for *Boundaries* by

- A finalist for the 2012 NAACP Ima

"Many moments of elegant, overarching insight bind the personal to the collective past."
—*New York Times Book Review* (Editors' Choice)

"A thoughtful literary novel exploring the shadows of cultural identity and the mirage of assimilation." —*Kirkus Reviews*

"Nunez deftly dissects the immigrant experience in light of cultural traditions that impact family roles, professional obligations, and romantic opportunities." —*Booklist*

"Ms. Nunez has always had the power to get to the essence of what makes human beings take right and wrong turns. With *Boundaries*, a reader will find that she, again, does not disappoint."
—Edward P. Jones, author of *The Known World*

"Elizabeth Nunez is one of the finest and most necessary voices in contemporary American and Caribbean fiction."
—Colum McCann, author of *Let the Great World Spin*

"A quiet, sensitive portrait . . . This work covers a lot of ground, from mother-daughter and male-female relationships to the tensions between immigrants and the American born."
—*Library Journal*

Critical Praise for *Anna In-Between* by Elizabeth Nunez

- Winner of the 2010 PEN Oakland Josephine Miles Award
- Long-listed for the 2011 IMPAC Dublin Literary Award

"A psychologically and emotionally astute family portrait, with dark themes like racism, cancer, and the bittersweet longing of the immigrant."

—*New York Times Book Review* (Editors' Choice)

"Nunez has created a moving and insightful character study while delving into the complexities of identity politics. Highly recommended." —*Library Journal* (starred review)

"Nunez deftly explores family strife and immigrant identity in her vivid latest . . . with expressive prose and convincing characters that immediately hook the reader."

—*Publishers Weekly* (starred review)

"A new book by Elizabeth Nunez is always excellent news. Probing and lyrical, this fantastic novel is one of her best yet. Fall into her prose. Immerse yourself in her world. You will not be disappointed."

—Edwidge Danticat, author of *Claire of the Sea Light*

"Nunez offers an intimate portrait of the unknowable secrets and indelible ties that bind husbands and wives, mothers and daughters." —*Booklist*

"Nunez's fiction, with its lush, lyric cadences and whirlwind narrative, casts a seductive spell." —*O, the Oprah Magazine*

"The award-winning author of *Prospero's Daughter* has written a novel more intimate than her usual big-picture work; this moving exploration of immigrant identity has a protagonist caught between race, class, and a mother's love." —*Ms. Magazine*

NOT FOR EVERYDAY USE

NOT
FOR
EVERYDAY
USE

ELIZABETH
NUNEZ A MEMOIR

Published by Akashic Books
©2014 Elizabeth Nunez

Paperback ISBN-13: 978-1-61775-233-9
Hardcover ISBN-13: 978-1-61775-234-6
Library of Congress Control Number: 2013956048

First printing

Akashic Books
PO Box 1456
New York, NY 10009
info@akashicbooks.com
www.akashicbooks.com

For Jason, Jordan, and Savannah

Acknowledgments

Johnny Temple is one of the finest publishers in America today. In this digital age when there are dismal predictions about the future of the printed word, he and his senior editor Ibrahim Ahmad are beacons of hope with their commitment to good literature and their courage not to be daunted by the naysayers. I am eternally grateful to them for their razor-sharp guidance with this book and two of my novels.

I had not thought of writing a memoir until I was persuaded to do so by the editors of the fine collection of essays *Shakespeare's Sisters*, and by my dear friend and poet Linda Susan Jackson. I thank them for opening up a world to me that I may have forgotten.

As always, my thanks to my son, Jason Harrell, for his love and support, and to his wife, Denise, and my sister Mary Nunez, who continually give me encouragement.

"Would you believe that I don't like to think
back on those times, primarily
because then I feel really sad,
really feel it, deep down?"

How can I answer her, who answered me
So many ways,
Whom now the same precocious spring betrays?
Say that time passes only to return?
Or utter that belated fiction that
Time saddens, true, but also makes us wise?

—Wayne Brown, "A Letter from Elizabeth,"
On the Coast and Other Poems

I

The phone rings. It is two in the afternoon. I am at home, in my house in New York. I am reviewing the final proof of my novel *Anna In-Between*. It's a novel I struggled to write, not because I couldn't find the words, but because I didn't *want* to find the words. It is the first of my novels that comes close to the bone, uncomfortably so. Mr. and Mrs. Sinclair, the main characters in the novel, are too much like my parents; the house they live in is exactly theirs.

I wrote this novel to unravel a mystery that had been hounding me. My parents had allowed a cancerous tumor to grow in my mother's breast for years so that it had reached the final stage, stage four, before my mother admitted its existence and my father acknowledged he knew. I was baffled and angry. Super angry. Why had my mother been willing to endanger her life, my father to risk it? Even now, as I review the edits my publisher has sent to me, I feel heat rising to my head.

But I am mixing fact and fiction. In reality, my mother lives. Her cancer may have reached the terminal stage, but it was not terminal. It is fifteen years now since my mother took the experimental drug that in six months reduced her tumor to a size that made surgery possible. Yet even then the tumor was huge. My brother, a surgeon, was in the operating room to witness the surgery.

"Mummy had more tumor than breast tissue," he told us. *The horror!*

I do not take *Anna In-Between* to the point when Mrs. Sinclair has a mastectomy. The novel ends when she agrees to have the surgery in the US. Her doctor offers her hope, hope that seems like a fantasy to Anna. Mrs. Sinclair will live to be ninety, Dr. Ramdoolal predicts. Mr. Sinclair grabs on to that prediction like a drowning man to driftwood. "Hear that, Beatrice? Live to be ninety!"

My mother was eighty-eight when I wrote that line, thirteen years after her mastectomy. She is ninety now.

Ninety! The number resounds in my head and my heart drops. I reach for the phone, but it has stopped ringing. In seconds, though, it rings again. I look at the caller ID: 868, the country code for Trinidad. I have many siblings; it could be one of them. My eyes skid over the rest of the numbers. My parents' phone number! But it would be my mother, not my father, who would dial the phone. My father has long ceded that responsibility to her. I brush away my foolish fears, my silly superstitions. *Mrs. Sinclair is not my mother. Dr. Ramdoolal is not her doctor. No one predicted my mother would live to ninety.* Then as quickly as relief flashes across my brain, my chest tightens again. We call our parents; they do not call us. They call us only on our birthdays. It is not my birthday. It is August, August 24. My hands are shaking when I lift the receiver, my heart pounding with every immigrant's fear: that call unexpected, on an unusual day.

"Hello."

No answer. Then my niece's voice, tremulous. "Granny." She is crying. The words that follow are muffled, convoluted.

"What's happened to Granny?" I ask, putting on a stern voice, my professorial voice. I want her to stop sniffling; I need to hear her clearly.

"You should come home now." She does not have to say more.

"Where is she?"

"In hospital."

"Is she . . ." I cannot get the words out. *Is she alive? Is she dying?*

"She's still breathing, but she can't talk. You need to come now."

My head spins, my heart races. I try desperately to calm myself down, but the more I try, the more my heart thunders through my chest. I dial my sister's number. Mary is the stoic one; Mary keeps her emotions in check. Only once have I seen her explode in anger or collapse in tears. I can depend on Mary's steady head to calm my nerves. The answering machine comes on and I remember Mary is not at home. She has gone on a cruise with her husband. The day before she left a terse message for me, Mary style. "I'm going on a cruise with Trevor to see the fjords in Alaska." That was all she said before she paused, and then I heard her take a deep breath. When she spoke again, it was to apologize. She did not mean to be brusque. "Sorry I didn't call you before. We just flew into Florida and will be leaving on the Holland America Line tomorrow."

It was August 23 when Mary left that message. It's August 24 now. Our mother is in the hospital. She cannot speak.

Mary is almost a decade younger than I am, but she is the practical one, the level-headed one, and now without her here to take charge of things, I panic. *Call the airlines*, I hear her voice in my head commanding me. *You need to get the first flight out of New York.* I am pulled full throttle into action. I dial Caribbean Airlines, the company that has taken over British West Indian Airways (BWIA), though I am told it still belongs to the government of Trinidad and Tobago. My uncle Mervyn was a captain on BOAC, British Overseas Airways Company, which once owned BWIA. His two sons are pilots; one of them is a captain on the recently renamed Caribbean Airlines. Two of my cousins are stewardesses.

"Sorry, but we have no seats," the ticket agent informs me.

I tell her about my mother. She sympathizes. She can get me on a flight in two days.

Two days will be too late. My gut and my heart tell me I must get home now. I use my trump card, the one that almost always works in the Caribbean. We are a collection of small islands; no neighborhood is so far from the other that it is not easily accessible: walking distance or by donkey and cart in the old days, by car on superhighways and a series of intertwining overpasses today. Our social network was in full gear before Facebook and Twitter. Everybody knows one of the somebodies you know, and if the somebody you are related to is important, doors open for you. I mention my uncle. His name makes no impression. The ticket agent is too young to remember my uncle. I mention my cousins, the pilots and the stewardesses. She knows them well. In an instant I have a seat, in first class no less.

By six o'clock the next morning, I am on my way to Trinidad. The stewardess has been told about my mother;

she knows why I am here, in first class. She whispers comforting words in my ear, something about how everything will work out. Something about praying for my mother. I reach into the zippered pouch where I keep my travel documents. My fingers slide across a circle of pearly white beads, ten of them; they form a small bracelet attached to a gold cross. It's a decade of the rosary. Mary gave the bracelet to me the last time we were traveling home together for our father's ninetieth birthday. I am terrified of flying. That so much metal can stay afloat in the air seems impossible to me, a mystery that defies my imagination, though for as long as I have known myself I have trusted my imagination to make sense of the world. My siblings tease that one should take everything I say with a grain of salt. They say I exaggerate outrageously. (Fair warning to you, Dear Reader!) One could cut in half all the stories Elizabeth tells, my siblings say. They claim I tell those stories as if they are the real truth. But my stories tell the real truth, the essential truth, I respond.

When I was a child, I refused to be limited by the reflections my retina sent to my brain. I would dress up the world in colors and with characters the ordinary eye did not see. I multiplied, I elaborated, I gave drama to the mundane. If there was a bicycle accident at the corner of the street where we lived—a too common occurrence—when I related the incident later, I embellished. Though the boy was hardly scratched, though he walked away, even laughed, when I told the tale there was blood in the gutter; there were tears, pitiful shrieks from his mother. The car that struck him was a shiny, enormous car, the man one of those official types you saw in the newspapers. The boy was a skinny, poor kid who had saved up his pennies bagging groceries at the local market to buy the bicycle he dreamed of. Now it was shattered and the man had driven away as if nothing had happened. What was the real truth I was trying to convey of these accidents that took place with regularity on our busy street? Life is unfair; the powerful do not care about the powerless; the good do not always win. There was more: Humans are vulnerable. Not only do adults die, children who have not yet reached pubescence can die too. *My mother and father can die. I can die.*

I think I was a writer before I became a writer. My imagination was my fuel. It fuels me now. Each time the plane rattles like loose metal in a tin cup as we pass through layers of sodden clouds, I am convinced I will not make it to Trinidad, or if somehow I do, my mother will not be alive when I arrive. My fingers tighten over the beads on the rosary bracelet. My mother had bought it for my father when they were in Italy, she to fulfill a lifelong wish to go to the Vatican, to see the pope, my father to see the ruins. My mother did not get to see the pope, but in the Vatican shop they sold her two rosaries they claimed were blessed by him: a silver circular metal one, no wider than half an inch in diameter, with a tiny cross on top, which she kept on her bedside table, and a bracelet of white beads with a gold cross, which she gave to my father. My father, a convert to Catholicism which he still did not fully understand, gave the bracelet to Mary and Mary gave it to me.

The hostess returns with a menu. She wants to know what I'd like to have for breakfast, what I'd like to drink. "A mimosa?" she asks. I am trying to remember the prayers of the rosary. *Hail Mary full of grace* . . . What is to follow? I have forgotten. I am staring at the hostess with a question on my face. She thinks she has made a faux pas. She claps her hand to her mouth. "Sorry," she says. I think she thinks she is being insensitive to offer me alcohol at a time like this, but it is at a time like this I need something to calm my nerves, my fear of flying, my fear of what I will find when the plane lands and I am home.

I roll my thumb over the beads of the bracelet. In my mind I repeat the first part of the Hail Mary. *Hail Mary full of grace* . . . I cannot remember the response. The hostess pats my hand. "It will be okay, you'll see," she says. And miraculously memory kicks in. It has been years but I remember it now. *Holy Mary, Mother of God* . . . I go through all the mysteries: the Joyful, the Sorrowful, the Glorious. The constant repetition eases me into a mindless trance, sleep overtakes me, and next I hear the pilot's voice. The plane has landed. I am home.

2

My sister Judith is at the airport. She has come in from St. Vincent where she lives with her husband Ian and her three children, Simone, Paige, and Cristine. By coincidence, our planes have landed within minutes of each other. My sister is punching numbers on an ATM machine. She is alone; her husband and children have not traveled with her. I call out to her and she waves, but she does not come toward me; she returns to the machine and punches more numbers before she turns back again and walks swiftly to me. We embrace. A kiss on the cheek, our arms enclosing each other in the second of that kiss. No tears. We are not a weepy family. We are Nunezes. We have been taught to keep our emotions in check. Emotions can be dangerous; they can derail you. But men and women who have survived marriages to my siblings have learned not to mistake our restraint for lack of commitment. One could get scorched coming too close to the firewall we build around each other.

My sister is an actuary; she deals in facts, in numbers that tell her the objective truth: how long a man may live; how much should be expended to keep him alive. She tells me the objective truth now. Our mother did not make it through the night.

I wanted to hold my mother's hand, even if she could

not speak. There was so much I wanted to tell her, so many years, so many blank pages between us since I left her home and my homeland for America, a mere teenager. I had been hoping she would be alive when I got to the hospital. I say this to my sister.

"The doctor proposed life support," my sister says, "but Mummy would have been a vegetable. She would not have wanted that. It's better this way."

I take in these facts. Still no tears come. I hook my arm in the crook of my sister's arm. She pats my hand briefly and we walk stone-faced toward the line of taxis.

My sister is incredibly beautiful. She looks like Halle Berry. She has her huge expressive eyes, high cheekbones, a sculpted face, and a wonderful wide smile. Judith is almost fifty; she could be taken for thirty, an older sister to her daughters. Three children and she still has an iron-board stomach. One child, and thirty years later I cannot lose the flab that drapes down at the bottom of my belly. Judith is petite; I am petite, but my sister's breasts, waist, and hips are perfectly contoured, her figure that of an iconic James Bond girl, Halle Berry emerging from the sea in an orange bikini.

Whenever I tell Judith this, she shrugs, shakes her head, and twists her mouth in a wry smile, politely dismissing my compliments as frivolous, inconsequential to her life as a mother and wife. Her world centers on her family, on her daughters and her husband, though she keeps a small part, which she protects fiercely, for her work as one of the few actuaries in the Eastern Caribbean. On the slope beneath the main floor of their house, Ian has built an office for her that opens to the garden and the swimming pool. From there she can do her work and still keep an eye on her daughters.

Ian is a wise man. He has known the Nunez family for years, ever since he was a teenager and his wife-to-be was a little girl in pigtails still playing with dolls. He understood the burning ambition sizzling beneath the domestic chatter of the Nunez women. The house he bought for my sister stands on top of a small hill with a magnificent view of the blue Caribbean Sea on one side and verdant cascading hillocks on the other. Judith is sensitive to the history of these hillocks. Once they were plantations where our ancestors were driven mercilessly under a brutal sun to provide the English with luxuries some boast of to this day without reference to their shameful past. Foreigners to our islands are amazed at how much we have achieved since those days, but what amazes my sister and me more is the horror, the inhumane cruelty of those who decimated the Amerindians and then brought Africans in chains to clear the land for sugarcane and bananas.

Inside the house, in the living room, Judith has created a comfortable space for her family with practical leather couches, fluffy pillows, side tables, a console with an enormous TV, and all sorts of electronic devices to entertain her daughters and husband. But the visitor has only to take a few steps down to the back of the house, to the office humming with computer equipment, shelves lined with bound files, an enormous desk and Madison Avenue desk chair to know that my sister has another life, one so carefully calibrated that it does not seep into the world she has created above it.

I notice that my sister is perfectly coiffed as if she has just come from the hairdresser's, which I know she could not have. I had no time to dye the line of gray that frames the front of my face. I had hastily put on a short-sleeved navy shirt-styled dress. It was the darkest summer dress I could find in my closet, five seasons old. My sister is wearing a perfectly fitted black linen skirt and a white designer blouse.

This is the sister who, though I know her heart is breaking, keeps a steady head and changes her EC currency for TT Dollars at the ATM at the airport so she won't have to rely on anyone. This is the sister who, though she sees me and waves to me, has the presence of mind to log out of the ATM before she races to greet me.

Self-reliance. It is another Nunez creed.

"No point in going to the hospital," my sister declares reasonably as I struggle to answer the taxi driver who has just asked for our destination. "Valsayn," she says to him, and to me, "We should go straight there. Daddy will be waiting."

Valsayn is where my parents built their last house, larger than they needed; nine of their children had already left home and the other two adult children were at university. My father is a family man. He was as devoted to his parents as he is to us. I once asked him why he took total responsibility for the financial support of his parents when he had eight siblings who could help. He answered: "Whether they do or not, that is their business. I want to be sure my parents have enough to live on." When he asked his friend, a famous architect in Trinidad, to design his house in Valsayn, he envisioned his children returning for holidays, his grandchildren spending long swaths of time with him. The house has four large bedrooms, and wide manicured lawns in the front and back, ample space where his grandchildren can play.

"Do you think Daddy knows?" I ask my sister.

"I'm not sure," she says.

We continue the drive to Valsayn in silence. Once or twice I look over at Judith. Her large eyes have widened to saucers. A deer in the headlights. I've seen that expression on her face before, too many times when her first marriage ended. I know my sister is terrified. I slide closer to her on the backseat. Our thighs touch.

I remember when Judith was born. My mother was forty-five. She would have fourteen pregnancies and nine live births by the time she reached menopause. We are eleven, but my first two siblings, my sister Yolande and my brother Richard, are not my mother's biological children. My father's first wife, Denise, died in childbirth. Two years later, my father married my mother, and ten months later I was born, so that within one year of her marriage, my mother was parent to an infant, me; a three year old, my sister Yolande; and a two-year-old, my brother Richard. The closeness in our ages made it easy for Yolande and Richard, as it did for the rest of my siblings, to think we were all children of the same parents. And we looked un-cannily alike, features from my father apparent in each of us. Some of us had his long nose, some his thin lips, some his piercing dark eyes, some his small bones, narrow hips, and flat backside. Only my mother's children had dark cir-cles under their eyes—raccoon eyes, my son calls them, as he too has inherited the genes passed on to my mother by her Carib forebears. My mother's eyes, though, were large and expressive and some of my sisters are lucky to have her eyes, not my father's, and her hourglass figure and not my father's slim frame. But when we were young and our bodies had not yet developed, there were sufficient features com-mon among us that we did not question our parentage.

Indeed, we all had another mummy, Mummy Denise. Every night we prayed for her. On All Souls Day, we put candles on her grave. I had no idea who she was. I thought perhaps she was an older, special friend of my parents who had died, though it was strange that we would refer to her as *Mummy* since we called all my parents' adult friends *Auntie* or *Uncle*. Yolande and Richard seemed uncertain of her identity too, or if they knew who she was they didn't reveal the truth to me. I was eleven years old before I knew otherwise. Some resentful relative on my father's side made the observation that I resembled my brown-skinned mother and Yolande resembled her "white" French Creole mother. I had certainly been aware that Yolande and Richard were light-skinned and I was butterscotch brown, but then I gave no special significance to that distinction, for my brother Wally, my mother's child too, was also light-skinned. Later, my father sat me down and explained the difference.

Though Judith is the last of my siblings, she was not the last of my mother's pregnancies. A rigidly orthodox Catholic, my mother was in mortal fear of God's punishment should she disrupt in His plan to populate the world. The rhythm method was the only means of birth control that the church approved, and, disastrously, still does, though only in the developing countries—in Africa, Latin America, and the Caribbean for example—does anyone pay much attention. The constitutional right to pursue their own happiness is far too ingrained in the psyche of most Catholic Americans. They reach for the loophole the church grudgingly admits: ultimately one should be guided by one's conscience. In countries like mine, however, the church has leeway to be dictatorial. After all, slavery and colonialism thrived for hundreds of years by exercising a stranglehold on the people.

I can still recall the chill that went through my body each time I saw my mother doubled over the sink and heard those retching sounds that continued morning after morning, year after year, as she vomited her insides. Another nine months of my mother irritable, frustrated, short-tempered with us, dark blue veins popping frighteningly along her legs. And after nine months, sleepless nights of a baby screaming in the room next to mine, diapers to wash, another child to babysit keeping me away from playing with my friends in the backyard.

My father found it impossible to convince my mother to use another method. The possibility of damnation in hell for all eternity terrorized her. I used to be frightened too of committing the smallest infraction on the interminable list of offenses the church had defined as sin, which could cause me to spend hundreds of years in purgatory or an eternity in hell. I was not quite seven, preparing to make my First Communion, when I found myself envying the cockroach. At least when it died, it died; there was no life for it after death, no possibility of burning in the fires of hell. Even at that young age, my list of sins was mounting: I had told a lie; I had stolen my brother's pencil; I had not done my chores. Already I was beginning to lose hope of heaven. I wonder now, as my sister Judith and I make our way to Valsayn, if in her last hours my mother found comfort in knowing she had faithfully obeyed God's commands as the church had dictated to her; if she found joy in believing that soon she would have her reward in heaven.

Three times my mother almost died. The first time she miscarried the doctor gave her a choice: the baby's life or hers. If the baby, she would bleed to death. The priest said the baby. The church said the baby. My mother, good Catholic, said the baby. My father was in the forest hunting with his friends. By God's grace, ironic as that sounds, he arrived back home in time. "My wife!" he yelled at the priest. "Have you all lost your minds?"

The rhythm method was too complicated for my mother. She was too exhausted at the end of the day to calculate the number of days before and after her period, to check her temperature for the right and wrong times to have sex with her husband. At first she improvised, devising a birth control method of her own. After my brother Roger was born, the tenth in the line of eleven, my mother found multiple reasons to have him sleep in her bed wedged between her and her husband. There was colic, there was the fear that my brother could suffocate in his crib in the sheet she had wrapped around him; my brother's constant crying only seemed to abate when he was snuggled against her warm skin. But this method could only be temporary. In a very short time my brother's limbs grew long. (In fact, at over six feet, he is the tallest of my siblings.) Soon his elbows and knees were digging into my father's side. My mother had to choose between a sleep-deprived, grumpy husband who was the only breadwinner of her family, or a spoiled child who could be easily subdued with another bottle of milk.

She tried abstinence, paradoxically almost as damning as artificial birth control, for she had been taught by her church that to deliberately deny her husband his conjugal privileges was also a sin. But she calculated that abstinence would only be a venial sin, some years of punishment in purgatory and then reprieve. On the other hand, had she used a contraceptive, she would have been condemned to eternal fires. I am convinced this was my mother's reasoning because one night I happened to overhear an argument between her and my father. My father had come home late, as he'd taken to doing for some months. He was drunk, or I think he was. I could hear my mother accusing him, shouting that she smelled perfume on him and it was not her own. "How could it be your own?" my father hissed. "You do not touch me."

My father never resented us though. He adored us. He celebrated each time one of us was born. He would brag to his friends, who wondered when the "string band of children" would end, that he had perfected birth control. The pattern of daughter followed by son had never failed, right through the eleven of us, notwithstanding the two children my mother had not given birth to or her five miscarriages. First there was Yolande, a daughter, and then Richard, a son; then Elizabeth (me), David, Jacqueline, Wally, Mary, Gregory, Karen, Roger, and Judith. My father would take bets when my mother went into labor. Every time he won.

Judith was named after St. Jude, the patron saint of lost causes. My mother had feared she would die giving birth to her. In the years between my birth and Judith's, my mother had had four miscarriages; the last miscarriage, like a previous one, had almost killed her. Still, following Judith there was another pregnancy. My mother was only months away from fifty by then. She had not had her period for three months. She was elated. Finally, menopause! Or so her women friends had told her. My father had to attend a business meeting in Canada and she decided to go with him and make a holiday of the trip.

My mother began bleeding the moment they got to the hotel. Within hours her condition was critical. The medics in the ambulance told my father that had he waited five more minutes to call them, they might not have been able to save her. It took liters of blood to get her pulse beating normally again.

Much has changed in the world yet women still die, or, like my mother, barely escape bleeding to death, because churches continue to terrify them with the fires of hell if they use artificial birth control. In times when AIDS wipes out almost entire villages in Africa, the Catholic Church continues to prohibit the use of condoms. There are places in the world where marriages are arranged to secure the financial stability of families, and young women, faithful to the church, are sent like lambs to the slaughter at the sacrificial altar to wed rich men who have indiscriminately indulged their desires for sexual pleasure and are likely to be carrying the virus. Today the women's movement has loosened much of the strangling control the church has had on women's lives, and few on my island have as many children as my mother had. My mother observed this turn of events with amazement. How was it that, with the exception of Yolande, who had three girls and one boy, none of her daughters had more than three children?

When I came to Trinidad, I always went to church with my parents on Sunday. We had just returned home from church one Sunday when my mother pulled me aside to ask me whether I had noticed that almost everyone at Mass had taken Communion. At first I thought her question was intended as a swipe at me. I had not taken Communion. I had remained sitting while the entire row in my pew stood up and walked to the altar. I was divorced and not celibate, sins according to the church for which, after years of agonizing, I now felt no guilt. Without repenting, I thought it would be both disrespectful and hypocritical to participate in a sacrament that requires repentance as well as belief in the transubstantiation of bread and wine into the body and blood of Christ.

"Oh, no," my mother said. "I wasn't talking about you. I meant *them*. Some of them have only one child."

How had they been so lucky? I could almost hear the question rumbling through my mother's mind. She had had no such luck. Her sex life had been constantly constrained by the fear of pregnancy.

In the 2012 US presidential elections, one of the candidates seeking the nomination of his party ran on a platform of social conservatism. Among his positions was his contention that birth control opened the door to promiscuous behavior. Without the controlling fear of pregnancy, women, he seemed to imply, would have a sexual field day whenever and with whomever they wanted. It seemed to me, though, that his argument had more application to the prohibition of premarital sex and adultery than to birth control. For if indeed artificial birth control opens the floodgates to wild unbridled sex, then for married couples I say: *Let the games begin!* But my parents had no such option, at least my mother did not, not with the full force of the Roman Catholic Church closing in on her.

Of course, my mother reassured me that she would not have wanted her life to be any different. She was grateful for every single one of us. We were all precious to her. But still.

"Could it be that there was something causing them to have miscarriages?" she asked.

I laughed. "You know better than that, Mummy."

And of course she did. Yet as farfetched as it was for my mother to entertain the possibility that there was an epidemic of miscarriages on her island, it was far more difficult for her to accept that the women in her church had used artificial birth control and yet had no qualms about receiving Communion.

"Mummy is in a better place," I say to Judith now, but I can think of no better place than the world we live in. I cannot imagine my mother ever consciously wanting to leave it.

> *O shining Odysseus, never try to console me for dying.*
> *I would rather follow the plow as thrall to another*
> *man, one with no land allotted him and not much to live on,*
> *than be a king over all the perished dead.*

So says Achilles, arguably the most ruthless of the great Greek warriors.

Judith smiles when I talk to her of a better place. She knows I am simply trying to console her. Like me, Judith is divorced from her first husband. Like me, Judith did not remain celibate after her divorce. Like me, when she went to church with my parents, she did not receive Communion. She embarrassed our mother as I embarrassed our mother when I remained seated as it seemed the entire church walked up to the altar.

According to our church, my sister is living in sin with her second husband. Thusly, too, her three beautiful daughters are bastards, a word I find difficult to roll off my tongue. Yet there it is, in the Oxford English Dictionary. *Bastard*: a person born to parents not married to each other.

Judith is not the only one of my sisters who was divorced and has remarried. Karen and Jacqueline also divorced their husbands and remarried, though Karen, like Judith, wanted children and had a child with her second husband. Technically, however, in the eyes of the church, Jacqueline was married only once. While her first marriage lasted twenty years and produced two children, the church found sufficient reason to declare the marriage contractually flawed and granted her an annulment so she could marry again as if for the first time.

I do not know if the decision of the church was influenced by the fact that Jacqueline had once joined a convent and was preparing to be a nun. She left the convent before she made her final vows and within months married her childhood sweetheart.

Better to marry than to burn, said Paul. Perhaps this was reason enough for the church's decision to annul Jacqueline's marriage, which seemed based on fear rather than commitment. I cannot be certain, for my sister has never discussed her annulment with me.

A better place. I return my sister's smile, but soon we turn away from each other and I can feel tears stinging the backs of my eyes. How is it possible to believe that the God who required my mother to bear more children than her womb could tolerate, who would have asked for the life of her unborn child in exchange for hers, how could I believe that this Catholic God who condemned two sisters' loving unions with their second husbands and bastardized their children while ironically bastardizing the children of another sister's first marriage by declaring that marriage null and void is the same God who so loves my mother that He has come to take her to a better place?

3

y father comes to the gate to greet us. His step is firm, spritely even, though he seems agitated, but there is no sign of that old man's shuffling he has adopted recently. Perhaps unfairly I say *adopted*, for he is ninety-three; he'll be ninety-four in less than three months. At his age he cannot be expected to control his ever-weakening knees. Most men at ninety have trouble even lifting their feet off the ground, and yet I say this resentfully. For my father has become Coetzee's slow man, one day pedaling his bicycle—I have a photograph of my father riding a bike at ninety-two—the next shuffling his feet through the corridors of his house. But my father has not suffered an accident. No one, nothing, has sent him flying up in the air to land stretched out on the ground. No one has carelessly lopped off a limb, a leg, because he is old and the old are practically useless. My father's limbs are intact. He has full use of them. Indeed, for a man of his age, my father is quite strong. Only two years ago, he would walk briskly to meet me at the iron gate that opens up to the driveway. Before my fingers could curl around the handles of my two suitcases, he would grab hold of both of them and carry them into the house, one in each hand, the muscles straining against his wiry leathered brown skin. "Leave him," my mother would say when I tried to help. "Your father is a strong man."

What made my father suddenly slow down? For many years there were signs that his mind was wandering, but still he remained a vigorous old man. Now he is a slow old man. What caused this change in him?

My mother claimed he woke up one day and *decided* he would not be a pawn in life's game. He would not give the Grim Reaper the upper hand. When the Grim Reaper came for him, he would be waiting. The Grim Reaper would not surprise him.

Perhaps she was right. Ever since he was a boy, my father depended on reason to find his way out of the most difficult of situations, but ultimately reason failed him. Reason could not answer the question that perpetually hounded him: Why does human life have to end? *His life have to end?* No matter how hard he tried, he could find no reasonable explanation. It made no sense to him that after years of working hard, gathering the wisdom that comes with experience, that his life should be snuffed out, come to a screeching halt. "So he decided to give up," my mother said, as if it were up to my father, to the power of his will, to determine how and when he would die.

On my recent visits back home—home being the place where my parents live—my father did not come hurrying out of the house to greet me. He walked toward me slowly, though his eyes twinkled with his happiness to see me. He did not bend to pick up both my suitcases at once. He took them one at a time. "Leave it there," he would say when I reached for the other one. "I'll come back for it." Old, tired, too often depressed, he was still a gentleman. "Humor him," my mother would say, sighing. "He's strong. He's only pretending to be weak."

And indeed my father was strong, *is* strong, as I can see now. For after allowing Judith and me to wrap our arms around his shoulders and kiss him on the cheek—he stays stock still as we do this—he picks up my suitcase in one hand and Judith's in the other.

Inside the house, he puts down our suitcases in the breakfast nook. Judith takes hers and disappears into the bedroom, and I am left alone with him. He is standing so close behind me I can hear each time he takes a deep breath and air rushes through his nostrils. "I have something to ask you," he says. I freeze. He wants to ask me what I cannot bear to say though I know he already knows. My sister Jacqueline, the second of my sisters, was in the doorway when Judith and I arrived. She whispered in my ear that our mother was alive when our brother Wally took my father home from the hospital. She has told my father that Mummy died soon afterward. He refuses to believe her.

I bargain for time. I tell my father that I need to go to the bathroom. "It's a long trip from New York to here," I explain.

He is unwilling to release me. "Wait," he says. His hand encircles my wrist.

Jacqueline comes out of the kitchen to rescue me. "Let Elizabeth go to the bathroom," she says to my father.

My father is still looking at me. "Did you hear me, Elizabeth?"

"Let her go," Jacqueline repeats, this time in a stern voice. My father steps away from me.

When I come out of the bathroom my father is standing outside, by the door, waiting for me. His beady black eyes are glistening, the muscles on the sides of his mouth twitching. Jacqueline is nowhere around.

"Daddy." I put my hand gently on his shoulder. "I'm so sorry. So sorry." He shrugs off my hand. The lift of his shoulder is swift, brusque. My hand drops to my side.

"They say Una is dead," he says without emotion.

They say. It is the reasonable man speaking, the man who has no patience with magical thinking, the man who seeks objective truths.

My father's eyes pierce mine. They are intelligent eyes, not at all the eyes of the shuffling old man my mother said he had decided to be. The twitching that began at his mouth has traveled down to his arms; his fingers thrum involuntarily against the side of his pants. I want to hug him but I know he would interpret my embrace as acknowledgment of his vulnerability. He would think I would think he was not *in compos mentis*, in full possession of his mind.

Not in compos mentis. When he was in the full vigor of his life, this was his patronizing dismissal of friends who disappointed him with the illogic of their arguments.

"Mummy did die," I say to my father as gently as I can. "She died last night."

"So they tell me," he retorts dryly. His eyes have not wavered from mine. He is the Grand Inquisitor. I am a child again. He wants proof. I must give him evidence that I am not lying.

"It's true," I say.

"If you say so . . ."

Jacqueline comes into the hallway just as I am muddling my way to an answer that I pray would deflect the pain from his eyes that is blinding me. "Come, Daddy."

She cups her hand over his elbow. "Petra has made your breakfast. It's getting cold."

I am saved by the clock. My father is a stickler for punctuality. It is past nine, an hour after he should have had his breakfast. He is momentarily distracted. "Where is Petra?" he asks irritably, looking around for her. Jacqueline guides him away from the bathroom door.

Petra is our parents' housekeeper. She is in the kitchen standing by the stove. She seems disoriented. She is rubbing her hands up and down the sides of her dress, her fingers clawing her thighs, her eyes glazed. Every morning, at eight o'clock sharp, Petra puts my parents' breakfast on the table. She has been told that my mother has died, but habit makes her set two places on the table: plates, cutlery, cups, and saucers.

She comes toward me the moment she sees me. "I don't know what to do, what to make for him," she says.

I put my arms around her and she leans her head against my shoulder. "Don't worry, Petra," I say. "Give him whatever you want."

She looks up at me red-eyed. "Every day Mrs. Nunez does tell me what to make for Mr. Nunez. Today I don't know." She is whimpering. No tears though.

"It doesn't matter, Petra. He'd like anything you make."

"I don't know if this morning he want hard-boil eggs or scrambled eggs." She twists her head back and forth. "I take a chance and make scrambled eggs, but he don't come. Now the eggs get cold."

"It's okay, Petra," I say, rubbing her back. "It's okay."

Petra is a jewel. She has the patience of Job, tolerating my father's demands without complaint. My father expects her to arrive at the house at seven o'clock sharp but will allow her to stay in her room until seven thirty. It is a room next to the kitchen, fitted with a bed, a chair, a bureau, and a cabinet for her clothes. It has its own bathroom and a door that opens to the back lawn. At seven thirty my father expects Petra to be at the stove preparing breakfast for his wife and him. If she is not out of her room by seven thirty, my father knocks on her door. "Mrs. Nunez and I can't be waiting for breakfast just because you want to primp up yourself, or because you went to a party last night," he says.

Petra is close to sixty; her hair has already grayed in the front and sides. She does not dye it. Yet she does not look old; she does not need to primp herself up. She is naturally attractive. Her polished black skin has retained its youthful glow; nothing sags on her body, not in her face or her neck or anywhere else where the flesh ordinarily loosens after fifty. Her waist has thickened and her hips have spread. Her figure cannot be said to be alluring, but more than once I have caught my father ogling her. My father—let it be said now—has an eye for beautiful women.

Petra does not have a boyfriend, at least I don't think so. Contrary to my father's accusation, it is unlikely Petra would be out partying late into the night. She has a son who is in his early forties. If she still has a relationship with her son's father, none of us know. Petra has never made reference to a man in her life. Whenever I have reason to go in her room—the ironing board and iron are kept there—I notice religious pamphlets on her bureau, but I do not think she belongs to any specific religion. Often while she cooks or cleans, she sings the old-time Anglican hymns that my grandmother loved: "A Mighty Fortress is Our God"; "Amazing Grace." A quiet comes over the house when she sings. My parents are Catholic, my mother Catholic at birth, my father a convert, but they both love the old Anglican hymns, our legacy I suppose from the colonial days when the English ruled our island. The English are gone now, but they had taught us these hymns in primary school, when we were children, impressionable, still young enough to love them without question and believe the stories they told us.

It bothers me that my father is so strict with Petra, so demanding. Petra dismisses my concerns for her. She loves my parents, she tells me. "They do things the old-time way. The world would be better if people did things the old-time way." She says young people today don't have respect for old people. "Everybody want to be in charge. Not everybody can be in charge. Some people know things better than other people. Your father knows things," she says. "I happy to listen to him."

It's hard to tell how much of Petra's attitude is owed to retentions of an African past when elders were revered, and how much to the legacy of colonialism with its strict enforcement of place on the rungs of the social ladder. Perhaps for Petra both hold true. She has held on to the traditions of her African ancestors, but she is also shaped by our island's history of centuries of forced obeisance and indoctrination. My father is not English, but he is her boss.

Now, before she greets my father, Petra swallows the tears that have begun to well in her eyes. "Morning, Mr. Nunez. You ready for your tea?"

My father pulls out his chair from under the table and sits down at his usual place, at the head. My mother's place is to his right. My father's chair has arms. The one at the other end of the table has arms too, but it is rarely used. There are no arms on the other chairs, none on the chair where my mother sits.

Petra serves my father his tea. She turns up his cup from the saucer, places two tea bags in it, and pours hot water from a steaming teapot. My father swivels his head to his right. My heart clenches. He is looking for my mother. He will not touch his tea until his wife has been served. He opens his mouth to speak, but no sound comes out. His bottom jaw hangs loose. "I forgot," he mumbles. His eyes lose their intensity. They turn dull as if a light switch has suddenly been shut off. He shakes his head and closes his mouth. He sighs, a deep intake of breath he seems reluctant to release.

"Una is still in the hospital," he says. He looks up at me. He wants me to confirm that it is true. I turn away. I do not have the heart to repeat that she has died in the hospital.

"Tea, Mr. Nunez?" Petra pushes the steaming teacup toward him.

He waves his hand over it. He does not want it. "I'm going to rest now," he says. He places his hands on the arms of the chair and rises slowly. He is the old man again, knees locked, joints cracking. Petra helps him up and he shuffles to his room.

Jacqueline tells me what happened the night before. Along with my sister Karen and my brother Wally, Jacqueline is one of only three of my siblings who still live in Trinidad. As she relates the details of my mother's last days and hours, the muscles in my chest tighten. I can hardly breathe. There were nights too when my chest constricted and I could barely breathe, but I was in America; I knew no one. I had to be strong.

My mother had been suffering with pains in her legs for some days, Jacqueline explains. "We gave her aspirins, but they didn't seem to help." She tells me she consulted with my doctor brothers. "Have her get off her feet," they said. "Have her rest." But my mother, bound by tradition and upper-middle-class conventions, continued to join my father at the table for breakfast, lunch, and dinner until on that fateful day, one week later, her legs still paining her, she got up abruptly from breakfast and went to her room.

My teenage niece was visiting. She was at the table with my nephew who was living at the time with my parents. Neither they nor my father seemed to think there was reason for alarm. What they probably thought was that my mother was finally following my brothers' advice and had gone to her bed. Almost half an hour later my niece found her sprawled on the floor. I cannot bear to describe her condition. How long had she lain there, paralyzed on one side, speechless? Suffice it to say, she had suffered a stroke, yet her remarkable brain was fully alert. When my nephew rushed to her side, she locked eyes with him. "What?" he asked, and her eyes rolled toward her night table. There she kept her prayer book and a crucifix, and next to them a round metal ring with raised beads welded into its circumference. *Her rosary.* My nephew knew immediately that this was what she wanted. When she was in bed, my mother was seldom without that ring hooked on her finger. I want to believe she was at peace then when my nephew placed the ring on her finger. I want to believe that she was consoled that the Virgin Mary, to whom she was devoted, was with her at that moment. *Holy Mary, Mother of God, pray for us sinners, now and at the hour of our death.*

My sister provides more details: how she, Wally, and Karen gathered around my mother's bed; how two of my parents' grandchildren were also there; how they sang hymns; how they recited my mother's favorite prayers; how they managed to reach Father Joseph, my parents' parish priest and their friend, who administered the sacrament of Extreme Unction to my mother.

"What about Daddy?" I ask. "What did he do? What did he say?"

"My God, how he loved her! Every woman should have a husband to love her like that." My sister, a widow, had gone through rough patches with her husband. She tells me now that my father stood close to my mother's bed, his hand resting on her paralyzed arm. From time to time he bent over her, his breath upon hers. "I love you, Una." His voice was clear, distinct, the old man's warbling he had recently adopted all vanished. "I love you more than I have ever loved anyone. I will go in your place. Tell God I am ready to go in your place. Do you want me to go in your place, Una?"

A question. My mother had neither the strength nor the voice to respond. My father loves life. He would never give it up willingly. My mother knew that. But it matters only that he said those words; it matters not that what he asked was impossible, nor that it was unlikely that if it were possible, he would have followed through.

4

How I envied my parents' marriage! Their marriage had lasted for sixty-five years, my paternal grandparents' marriage even longer. When my grandmother died, she had been married to my grandfather for seventy years. My marriage fizzled after two years, but I stayed for eighteen more, twenty in all by the time I filed for divorce.

In my kitchen, next to my stove, where I cannot miss it, I keep a framed photograph of my grandparents on the day of their seventieth wedding anniversary. They are standing next to each other, arm in arm, a proud man and his equally proud wife. They have accomplished much and they know it. My grandfather leans slightly toward my grandmother. It is obvious that he loves her, but my grandfather's love for my grandmother was not the same as my father's love for my mother. My father's love for my mother remained suffused with sexual passion. My grandfather's love for my grandmother was the love for a partner who had travelled with him through life and worked side by side with him to raise nine successful children. In the photograph, my grandmother is holding a bouquet of flowers that trail down the diaphanous dress she is wearing. She is smiling, a deceptively winsome smile, I think. Deceptive, for in spite of the flowers, the dress, the coquettish smile, she is standing erect, her head held high, the strong and determined woman I knew her to be.

I do not have a photograph of my great-grandparents together, but I have seen a photograph of my great-grandfather. It was dated sometime in the second half of the 1800s. My great-grandfather, Antonio Nunes, was Portuguese, from the Madeiras. He was ten years old when his father brought him to Trinidad with a group of Portuguese who were seeking their fortunes in the British West Indian colonies.

My older brother Richard claims, however, that our great-great-grandfather had not left Madeira voluntarily. He says that Antonio Nunes belonged to a family of Jewish mathematicians who lived on the islands of Ibiza, which, in the time of the Christian Inquisition, were a sanctuary for Jews fleeing persecution and torture. In the fifteenth century, when European kingdoms were competing with each other for land in the New World, Prince Henry the Navigator of Portugal recalled Peter Nunes (Petrus Nonius was his Latin name) from Ibiza. Prince Henry had ambitions for conquering the coast of Africa and needed the skills of mathematicians to develop instruments that would allow his navigators to see land far beyond the seas. In those days mathematicians were, and perhaps are still today, the best geographers, and Peter Nunes was the most famous of the Portuguese mathematicians.

Among the first lands the Portuguese found with the help of Peter Nunes were the Madeiras, and as a reward for his invaluable assistance, Prince Henry allowed him to settle his Jewish family there. The family converted to Roman Catholicism and continued to serve the Portuguese kings, but eventually not even their superior skills in mathematics, or their willingness to join the Catholic Church, were enough to spare them from the Portuguese persecution of the Jews. Years later, my great-great-grandfather's family was among the Catholic Jews, who, tormented by the accusation that the Jews were to blame for the crucifixion of Jesus Christ, converted to the Presbyterian Church, attracted to the charismatic Scottish Protestant missionary Dr. Kalley, who preached a more tolerant gospel. Then, in the 1840s, the Catholic majority in Portugal revolted against the heretical Presbyterians. The Presbyterian Jews fled in terror to the West Indies where they were promised religious freedom.

There may be some validity to this history. My great-grandfather was Presbyterian, not Catholic, as were most Portuguese, and the story of my family's lineage may account for our inclination toward the mathematical and natural sciences, though that gene bypassed me. I was more than an average student in mathematics but it held no interest in me. Literature was, and still is, my love, my passion. Stories well written, well told, fill my life with joy. My father, however, loved the sciences. He was an excellent student in chemistry, physics, and biology, and when he sat for his A-level Cambridge exam his score in his physics exam was almost perfect. The adjudicators, however, questioned the validity of his results. It was impossible that one could have such a perfect score! But my father had a photographic memory. Even into his late seventies he was capable of recalling almost to the letter something he had read. To the day she died, my grandmother never forgave the British colonial office for doubting her son.

The mathematical and science genes (if my brother's theory is correct) were also passed on to most of my siblings. Three of my brothers—David, Gregory, and Roger—are physicians. Roger was an engineer before he switched to medicine. A brother and a sister—Richard and Judith—are actuaries. Three sisters—Jacqueline, Mary, and Karen—hold MBA degrees. (Karen is also a lawyer). Another sister, Yolande, is a nurse.

The old Jewish dentist I used to go to when I first settled in New York in the late '60s also had a theory about my possible Jewish lineage. He was curious about my surname. He could not understand why I should have a Hispanic name though I am not Hispanic. I told him that my family's original name was Nunes. My grandfather had changed it to Nunez after an argument over the John Keats poem "On First Looking into Chapman's Homer," which all elementary school children on our island were required to memorize.

My grandfather was the headmaster of the only school in a forested area in the middle of Trinidad. He'd had a classical education in the old colonial schools in Trinidad. He had studied Greek and Latin, and even after he graduated from secondary school, he continued to be tutored in classical Greek. Homer's *Iliad* and *Odyssey* were his favorites. I too had studied Homer in secondary school, though by then Greek was removed from the curriculum. (Latin through forms one to five remained.) In my classes we read George Chapman's translation of Homer, which Keats had praised, except in his poem Keats had made a mistake. It was not the "stout Cortez" with his "eagle eyes" who first "star'd at the Pacific"; it was the great Vasco Núñez de Balboa. Miffed that the British colonial ministry of education, which determined the textbooks for the schools, would allow children in the West Indies to be confused by Keats's error, my grandfather promptly changed his name to Nunez in protest. All his children followed suit, except his second son, Winston, who was light-skinned and already under the wings of Presbyterian missionaries from Canada who promised to take him there. In Canada, my uncle found it easier to pass as a white man with the name Nunes rather than Nunez. He became a famous minister of an extensive evangelical congregation, married a white Canadian woman, and had "white" Canadian children. Neither his wife nor his children ever set foot in Trinidad during my grandparents' long life.

The dentist had asked me for photographs of my grandfather and father, and after examining them, he declared that they both had the Jewish nose, and except for the color of their skins, they could pass for Jews, my father a dead ringer for Saul Bellow, he said. If I had the photograph of my great-grandfather Antonio Nunes to show him, the dentist would have had more ammunition to support his conviction. But after my grandmother died, the photograph of my great-grandfather strangely disappeared. It had hung in the corridor of my grandparents' house for years, that photograph of a Portuguese man with a perfectly trimmed black mustache and a long, curved nose.

"*You* have the nose too," the dentist declared.

My nose is not as long or curved as some of my brothers' noses, but I am often taken for South Asian Indian or Arab or Ethiopian. After 9/11, my brother Gregory had to shave off his beard. His resemblance to a relative of

Osama Bin Laden was too strong. But no one had ever said that any of us looked Jewish. The dentist was certain though. "Of course your surname had to be Nunes," he said. "I know it could not be Nunez. Nunes is a good Portuguese Jewish name."

Whether my great-grandfather Antonio Nunes was Jewish or not, I cannot say for certain, but I do know he married an African woman, Ann Rose Dormor, the daughter of a freed slave.

Slavery had been abolished in 1834 in the British colonies, ending hundreds of years of free forced labor by Africans but leaving the plantation owners desperate for workers for the sugarcane and cocoa plantations. The British colonizers raked their colonies in China and India, promising passage back to the homeland or five acres of land to anyone who was willing to enter a contract of indentured labor for five years. They sought Europeans too. The imbalance between the white and colored populations in the West Indian colonies was too severe, too threatening. There were too few of them, too many blacks. What if the blacks revolted? So they promised Europeans large swaths of land on the islands if they would emigrate.

When the Portuguese first came to Trinidad they were so poor and so unsophisticated that even the black people did not consider them white. But it did not take the Portuguese long to realize that in the colonies their skin color was worth money, and there was much to gain by aligning themselves with the British colonizer. They established the Portuguese Club in Port of Spain, the capital of the island, and banned all people of color from membership. In other words, the Portuguese decided to become white. James Baldwin, the African American writer, would observe a similar phenomenon in the United States. Jews, he was reputed to have said, did not become white until they immigrated to America where blacks were the ones who were persecuted.

Antonio Nunes could have come to Trinidad simply to make his fortune, and not, as my brother Richard claims, to escape anti-Semitism in Portugal. But if indeed he was one of the Portuguese Presbyterian Jews who had converted out of fear of persecution, it seemed he had decided not to throw in his lot with them. Unlike many of the Portuguese, he did not go into the grocery business; he chose instead to work on the cocoa plantation. It was there his Portuguese son Antonio Nunes Jr. met my great-grandmother, Ann Rose Dormor.

Ann Rose Dormor's father had been enslaved, but when he was emancipated, he made sure that his only daughter was educated. Every day he drove her by horse and buggy from Arouca in the east to Port of Spain in the west, two hours each way, most of the trip on unpaved dirt roads, so she could go to Tranquility, the only school for black people that went beyond the elementary level. So we know that Ann Rose valued education. When her husband died, she made certain that her children were educated. One son, who kept the name Nunes, was an organist and a pianist. He immigrated to the US in 1919 to join the Louis Mitchell jazz band and was still a member when they played at the Casino de Paris in France. Later, he became a successful dentist in Harlem. Another son was my grandfather, Antonio Nunes/Nunez, who was a school headmaster and a forest warden.

That the Portuguese man married my great-grandmother, an African woman, rather than live with her without the sanction of the law or the blessing of the church, as was common between a white man and a black woman, was a source of pride in our family. With such forebears, with great-grandparents whose marriage lasted until the death of my great-grandfather, with my grandparents' as well as my parents' many-decades-long marriages and their commitment to family, how could I have ended my marriage after two years even though I knew then it was doomed? How could I have pulled my son away from the home where his father lived? I'd had the good fortune to grow up with my father in our home; my father had had the same good fortune, and his father the same. So I stayed in my marriage until my son left for college. But I had no point of reference in my own life to know the kind of love a man could have for his wife that would lead him to offer his life for hers, even if in the depths of his heart he hoped he would not have to make such a choice. I did not have my mother's good luck.

Years later my son, riddled with guilt, would wonder if he had robbed me of the chance to find such love. I told him what my father had told my siblings and me: we had not asked to be born; he and our mother had chosen to have us. They were responsible for us, not the other way around. They owed us; we didn't owe them. Still, I was envious of my parents' good luck, their long-lasting marriage.

5

I am alone in the den, sitting on the sofa, sipping the fourth cup of tea I have had since I arrived a mere hour and an half ago. Jacqueline and Judith have gone to the funeral home to make the arrangements for my mother's burial. My eyes are trained on the TV in front of me though I neither hear nor see what is on the screen. My head is in a fog, the impossibility of my mother's absence blocking every other thought or sensation from entering my brain. This is my mother's home. I am in her house, her den, watching her TV. How could the house exist without her! It is a cruel joke that bricks and mortar have longer lives than we, breathing intelligent beings. How they mock us, we who were their creators!

I do not hear when Petra comes to the den until she speaks: "She tell me thank you."

I turn to face her. Her polished skin shines in the startlingly bright sunlight pouring through the kitchen door and down the corridor to the entrance of the den where she is standing, her face stiff with grief.

"She tell me so last night. I don't mean yesterday before she had a stroke and can't speak. She tell me the night before. I was getting ready to leave and she come in the kitchen and say, *Thank you, Petra, for all you did for me. God bless you.* I loved Mrs. Nunez, don't mind she sometimes get over fussy with me, but I loved her. Yes, that is what she did. She say, *Thank you, Petra*."

Petra's eyes are open wide, as if propped up by invisible wires. She too cannot believe my mother is not here to fuss with her, to complain that the eggs she made in the morning are too hard, that there was dust in the corners of the corridor that she missed when she swept the day before. The film of moisture across her eyes glistens, but like me, she does not let the tears fall.

What is it about us Trinidadians? Did we inherit the British fears too, the stiff upper lip meant to suppress hysteria inevitable if one surrenders oneself to the onslaught of one's emotions?

Or was it insanity we feared, that old canard about black magic in the Caribbean, about the tropical sun heating up the blood?

The novelist Jean Rhys, a white Creole from the English West Indian colony of Dominica, would feel compelled to defend her people against that lie. In her novel *Wide Sargasso Sea*, Rhys takes on Charlotte Brontë, not at all persuaded to sympathize with Rochester, the Englishman who imprisons his white Creole wife, Bertha, in the attic. His wife had gone mad, Brontë's Rochester explains to Jane Eyre, the pure Englishwoman. And Brontë leaves it to the reader to assume that it was Bertha's West Indian upbringing that had brought on her madness.

Not so, says Rhys. It is Rochester who drove Bertha mad, not the West Indies. When West Indian critic Wally Look Lai asks her why she wrote *Wide Sargasso Sea*, Rhys is unequivocal: "The mad wife in *Jane Eyre* always interested me. I was convinced that Charlotte Brontë must have had something against the West Indies, and I was angry about it. Otherwise, why did she take a West Indian for the horrible lunatic, for that really dreadful creature? I hadn't really formulated the idea of vindicating the mad woman in the novel but when I was rediscovered I was encouraged to do so."

And yet I cannot deny the rumors about my mother's family. My father watched us closely as we were growing up. I was the first child he had with my mother, so he kept a particularly close eye on me. I was a nervous child, he seemed to believe. I am told I cried a lot when I was a baby; perhaps I suffered from colic. I know I had a sensitive stomach. I was all of ninety-seven pounds when I was nineteen, the year I first came to America. But I wasn't a nervous child. I was an anxious child, anxious to please a father looking for fissures in the mask I wore to conceal my emotions and a mother needing to prove there wouldn't be any. To get their approval, to put them at ease, I learned early to control outward expressions of my feelings, as I do now, remaining dry-eyed though it is mere hours since I learned of my mother's death.

But what about Petra? I doubt she had such demons in her family history. She stands in front of me, wreathed in grief, her eyes boring into mine, no tears, her bottom lip clenched between her teeth. She releases her lip only to repeat, "I did love her."

Did the British teach Petra to repress her emotions? Did they persuade us all with their talk about character, about how character distinguishes man from beast, about how the beast has no control over its reactions, but man, on the other hand, uses reason to suppress the passions?

If the exuberance of our steel pan music, the sensuality of our calypsos, the raucous abandonment on display on the streets during our Carnival celebrating our joy in being alive, in being human, are any evidence, then surely the colonizers have failed miserably. Surely we know that to be human is to think *and* to feel. Surely we know that character is not shaped by the unnatural denial of emotions but by values such as integrity, compassion, justice. By our emotional response to the cold, steel edge of cruelty.

Still, there is something about Trinidadians which crosses all levels of social class. Behind stone faces, behind the wide grin, behind the stoicism that Petra now displays, is a dam. When it fills to the brim, it explodes. Then run for cover if you are in the way of the people's fury, their scorn, their grief.

6

Petra returns to the kitchen. Minutes later I hear the creak of my father's bedroom door opening. He hasn't been able to sleep. I take a deep breath and wait, anticipating his insistent demands for proof. My mother was alive when he left the hospital. He won't believe she is dead unless he has proof, unless he sees her lifeless body.

He is dressed in a tuxedo, the broad lapels on the jacket gleaming, the silken ribbon running down the sides of the pants reflecting the bright morning sun. "Daddy," I say, alarmed, "what is it you have on? Where do you think we are going?"

He looks at me bewildered, and suddenly my mind skitters to the time, mere months ago, when I had seen him wearing the very same tuxedo. I was in my parents' home, sprawled out in shorts and tank top on a cushioned chair in the veranda, beaten down by the midafternoon heat. My mother had come running toward me, panting for breath, her face flushed. "Come, help me, Elizabeth. We have to get your father dressed." She wanted him to go with her to the funeral of a man they knew who was active in their parish church—but my father, like me, was taking his afternoon nap.

Is this the day my father is remembering, the day my mother helped him dress for a funeral? Is this why he is wearing the tuxedo? Have my words finally penetrated his brain, found a slit in the crust that has been imprisoning his memory? "Mummy did die," I had said to him. "She died last night." Has he finally accepted his wife is no longer alive, that she will not be coming home? Not ever?

I had followed my mother into her bedroom that day. My father was curled up in the bed, his chest rising and falling softly with each breath he took. I did not want to disturb him. "Tell him he has to get up, Elizabeth," my mother commanded when I hesitated. I knew that tone, that stern voice she used, and those lips, the top one clenched stiffly over the bottom one, deepening the ridges that cut down the sides of her mouth to her chin. I was over sixty years old, but that voice and that lip still had the power to propel me into action. It amazes me as I write this that at my advanced age I would have allowed my mother to intimidate me, but it is not age that severs the umbilical cord that links child to parent; it is death. So long as my mother was alive, I was her daughter, her child.

I did my best to coax my father into sitting up. My mother was already riffling through his closet. "Here, Waldo." She handed him a pair of pants. "Put this on." It was the pants to a tuxedo outfit, the silk stripe down each leg shimmering against the dull black fabric. I could have told her then that a tuxedo is the wrong suit to wear to a funeral, but she would already have known that. She was in a hurry. Her hand had fallen on the first dark suit in my father's closet. She didn't have time to correct her mistake, to wait for him to change his clothes.

My mother was one of the most stylish women I knew. Even in the days when my father struggled to put food on the table for a wife and their ten children (Judith was not yet born when money was scarce in our family), my mother was always fashionably dressed. She had an uncanny sense of style and could wear her skirts, tops, and dresses in such different ways that it was difficult to tell how few clothes she actually had. On Parents' Day, I couldn't wait for her to come to my school. She was always the best dressed of the mothers. But that day when my mother handed my father a tuxedo to wear to a funeral, being fashionably dressed was the last thought on her mind.

"Come on, Waldo," she hurried my father along. "I don't want to be late. We have to leave now . . . Elizabeth! Elizabeth, let's go now!"

Did she expect me to drive them to the funeral? My mother knew how to drive, though she had not been behind the wheel of a car in more than fifty years. My father had taught her out of necessity. He had just been promoted in the colonial office of the Ministry of Labour, and it was difficult for him to find the time to take my mother shopping. One day, just months after my mother got her license, he decided to drive with her down Frederick Street to test her skills. Frederick Street was then the busiest street in our capital city, the epicenter of our department stores, fancy offices, and restaurants. From the moment my father got into the car he began haranguing my mother, as he usually did, about all the mistakes she was making. She was either going too fast or too slow; she hadn't seen a pedestrian crossing in front of her, or she hadn't stopped firmly enough at a stop sign. My mother did not say a word, but at some point she'd had enough. She stepped on the brake and the car came to a screeching halt in the middle of the road. Drivers honked their horns behind her. It was midafternoon and the sun was brutal. Air-conditioning in cars was not yet common on our island. "Move your car, lady!" the drivers shouted angrily. My mother ignored them. She opened the car door, got out, and without a word slipped into the backseat.

I imagine my father was totally shocked, but more than that, he was mortified. They were in the middle of Port of Spain. Some of his friends and coworkers had surely been witness to my mother striding haughtily out of the car and my father sliding sheepishly over to the driver's seat.

How many times had I wished I had the courage to do what my mother had done, not just to stuff the mouth shut of some quarrelsome person, but to punish him as well!

Now, my father is standing in front of me, dressed in a tuxedo to go to see his wife. "Are you ready to take me to the hospital?" he asks.

I get up and switch off the TV. Will I tell him he has to change his clothes? Do I have the courage to say that his wife is not in the hospital? I can feel him behind me. I know if I turn around I will be a hair's breath away from him. I step to the side and fiddle with the books on the shelf above the TV. When I do not answer him, my father says irritably: "You can drive, can't you?"

He knows I know how to drive, and though his question is probably innocent, once again I am flung backward in time, to another age when I was a teenager on the verge of adulthood. My father has taught my older sister and brother to drive. David, the brother under me, teaches himself. When it's Jacqueline's turn, the sister younger than David, my father teaches her too. He does not teach me. I am under scrutiny. He is looking for signs that the genes from my mother's family have not been passed on to me. He cannot be sure I have nerves steady enough to maneuver my way through Trinidad's narrow two-way streets, or whether my reflexes will be sharp enough to avoid colliding with the oncoming traffic.

I had to come to America to learn how to drive. I was in my late twenties, living in New York, when I finally got my license. I had failed the test three times. My confidence had been so destroyed by my father's lack of faith in me that each time I took the test my knees shook uncontrollably and my hands dripped with sweat. Once, I was so nervous I backed into a mailbox. The fourth time I took the test, I confessed my problem to the inspector. He took pity on me and passed me. Today I drive confidently in traffic in New York City and on the parkways and expressways. I have never had an accident.

Now, faced with my father's question, I am nervous again. Perhaps it is true: I do not have the nerves to navigate the streets in Trinidad. I am uncomfortable with a steering wheel on the right side of the car, uncomfortable with traffic passing me on the right, uncomfortable with the open ravines that drop dangerously from the sides of some of the city's older streets. But mostly I realize, to my chagrin, to an unease that makes me peevish, that it is *he* who makes me nervous; it is the thought of *him* sitting next to me, judging me, testing me, that sends a slight tremor rippling across my right eyelid.

"Because if you can't drive," my father adds, looking at me with the determination of a man who has made up his mind to do what he wants, "I can drive. My car is in the driveway."

And indeed his car has been in the driveway ever since he finally conceded that he ought to surrender the keys. He is a stubborn man, though not unreasonable. He will not do something simply because he is told to do it, but he will consider the legitimacy of a request and if it has value, he will comply in his own way and in his own time. He was ninety when he stopped driving. We had been urging him to stop years before then. He had been able to pass an annual physical that the department of motor vehicles required by having his friend, who was also his physician, sign off on his health forms. "I don't ask Paddy to do any favors for me," he said, when we questioned the validity of the tests. "Paddy has me read the eye charts. I take him for a drive. He knows I know left from right." Then Dr. P. died suddenly of a heart attack. "See," my father said, smirking. "Paddy was what, fifteen, eighteen years younger than me? What difference does age make? I'm here; he's gone."

My father was finally convinced to get from behind the wheel when Jacqueline appealed to his sense of morality. "It's not just about you, Daddy," she said. "What about the other person who could get hurt because your reflexes are not strong enough to avoid them or to stop the car on time?" The next day my father announced that he would no longer be driving, but he refused to sell his car or give it to one of his grandchildren. He would keep it in the driveway just in case.

And going to the hospital to see his wife is just such a case.

I decide to be firm. I am a grown woman; he is an old man. He cannot intimidate me. *Because if you can't drive . . .* What does he mean to imply? I have been driving for years. In busy metropolitan New York City no less!

"I can drive you," I say harshly, a bit too harshly I realize when the words fall back on my ears.

His eyes brighten. "You know your way to the hospital?"

I am immediately remorseful. I cannot deceive him; I cannot allow him to hope. "Mummy is not in the hospital," I say, my tone softer.

He turns away from me.

"After you left the hospital . . ." I stumble and try again. I make myself say the words. I summon up my mother's courage. "After you left the hospital, Mummy died."

He puts his hands on his knees and lowers his body down on the couch in the den. His face turns gray; the twitching returns to his temples; his mouth is slack.

"I'll take you to see her." I sit down beside him.

"In the funeral parlor?" He looks up at me, his eyes begging me to lie, to give him the answer he wants. *No, not there. I made a mistake. I meant the hospital.* But I steel myself.

"Yes. In the funeral parlor," I reply. His head drops, chin grazing his chest. I put my arms around his shoulders. His body is unyielding, but he does not move away. "I'll call," I say. "I'll ask if I can take you to see her now."

I call. The owner of the funeral parlor is gracious, but she explains that she is not ready to have my mother's body viewed. It is early afternoon; my mother died in the early hours of the morning; she received her body less than an hour ago. "Come tomorrow morning," she says. "We'll have her ready by then."

My father takes the news without resistance. His pace is slower and unsteady as he goes back to his room. He shuts the door behind him.

7

We have to find our sister Mary. In the confusion of the day, I remember her message only partially. I remember she is on a cruise to Alaska, but I have forgotten the name of the ocean liner.

"When did she leave?" Jacqueline quizzes me.

"On the voicemail she said 'tomorrow.'" I startle both of us with my answer. *Tomorrow is today. Mary is already on her way to Alaska!*

Mary is an intensely private person, which is not to say that she and I are not close. As I was to discover in the process of writing *Anna In-Between*, privacy is not the same as intimacy. Mary and I are intimate friends though we weren't always so. We live near each other in Long Island, New York, twenty minutes apart, and are in constant contact. Still, there are days when I do not hear from her, sometimes for a week or more. I do not intrude; she will not allow me. I must wait until she resurfaces, as she always does. So I was only vaguely aware of her plans to go on a cruise to Alaska.

Mary was eighteen when my mother sent her to me in New York. She arrived all skin and bones, gangly legs, long arms, hardly any hips. But she was pretty, prettier than I ever was or would be, and taller, skin polished black with hints of red shimmering through, nose sloping gently, lips neither too thick nor too thin, and none of the dark circles under her eyes most of us inherited from our mother. Judith, who was still a young child then, would grow up to be a beauty. She would exude a sexuality that was more restrained in Mary, but Mary turned more than one head with her pretty face.

I was twenty-four when Mary came to live with me. I had graduated from college and landed a job as a caseworker with the Department of Social Services, a position available to even the greenest of college graduates in those days, the late '60s. The Vietnam War was raging; on TV, body bags with America's fittest—young men, mostly young men, but young women too—rolled out of cavernous cargo planes, night after night for everyone to see. Fewer and fewer left to teach the children, to care for the poor and the elderly. You walked into the Department of Social Services, took a routine test that proved you knew how to read, and in two weeks you had a job. Caseworker.

Soon I was able to rent an apartment and buy a car. My mother was convinced I was now in a secure position to take responsibility for my younger sister. And that was true. I had a green card, that enviable conduit to citizenship in America. I was a legal immigrant, permitted to earn my living in America. Mary arrived with a temporary diplomatic visa to work as a secretary in a clerical department at the UN.

How I was able to get a green card so easily and so quickly within months after I graduated from college remained a mystery to me for years, until, like the parts of a jigsaw puzzle, I snapped into place the loops and tabs that connected the events in America in 1965 to the tragedies of 1968.

In 1965, the year after the Civil Rights Act became law, Congress passed an amendment to the Immigration Act striking down country of origin as a criterion for immigration. This meant no longer did Northern Europeans have the special advantage of larger immigration quotas than other countries, particularly countries where the vast majority of the population were people of color. But it would take more than a law to change the hearts and minds of people who conceived of America as the land for the descendants of white Europeans (regardless of the fact that Native American Indians were here before the first European arrived). It took the assassination of Martin Luther King, Jr. on April 4, 1968, followed in two short months by the murder of Robert Kennedy on June 5, to stir the consciences of most Americans. When, in the summer of 1968, I applied for a green card at the US embassy in Trinidad, there was an embarrassing backlog of applications that had been put on the shelf by an administration reluctant to permit people of color into the US. Now, with the eyes of the world upon America for its treatment of its black citizens, the immigration officer was shamed into complying with the law. He asked few questions. He simply confirmed I was not a criminal and stamped my passport with a visa for permanent residency.

So I had this advantage over Mary when she arrived in New York. Perhaps I was not sensitive enough to her tenuous position in America; perhaps I acted as if I were a worldly, sophisticated New Yorker without a care in the world—but I was pretending and Mary resented me for my attitude. In time, though, she exacted her revenge, fine-tuning her game of one-upmanship, giving me hints of information and withholding the rest, letting me know she was the one holding all the cards. She was still playing her game two days ago, which is why I am angry with her now for not giving me the full details of her trip to Alaska.

But when Mary came to live with me in New York, I was no less green than she was. I had been forced to grow up. I had met a young man. I had fallen in love. I had had my heart broken.

I met F— in my senior year at Marian College, a small liberal arts school in Fond du Lac, Wisconsin, a place we in Trinidad would have described as "behind God's back." As indeed it was. There were less people in that town than there were in the city I had left in Trinidad. And there were no black people in it. No people of color of any type, in fact, except for three other girls in the college, all like me on scholarship, two from Haiti and one, an Indo-Trinidadian, Pat Ramdeen, who remains my dear friend to this day. Though much of what takes place in my second novel, *Beyond the Limbo Silence*, has little basis in the facts of my life, the events that led to Sara's arrival at the fictitious College of the Sacred Heart pretty much detail how I ended up in Fond du Lac, Wisconsin.

Against the prevailing odds, I became student government president, my ascendancy mirroring the rise of Putney Swope, the only black member of an all-white board of directors of an advertising company in the eponymous 1969 movie. My election, however, put the administration in a quandary. How to attract the daughters of well-heeled Catholic Midwesterners if the president of the student government is black? At the time the college had a lot to boast about. It had just completed construction on a new chapel with an unusual beehive exterior. The administrators wanted to show it off and thank their donors. But how to do that? In the end, they developed a glossy brochure with a photograph of the chapel. There are some girls milling around the front of the chapel. The president of the student government is nowhere in sight.

But I could not be denied the right to represent the students at the major conference of Catholic colleges held in Madison to discuss the mushrooming student protests against the Vietnam War. F— was president of the student government at Fordham University, so he was there too. We were instantly attracted to each other. By the time I left Madison to return to my college, I had a boyfriend.

All through our senior year, F— and I wrote passionate love letters to each other and made whispered telephone calls at night. F— says that the first time he was on a plane was when he came to visit me in Fond du Lac. After we graduated, F— went to Yale Law School and I returned to Trinidad with the intention of coming back to New York for graduate school, but really to be with F—. Again, there were the passionate letters, the frequent overseas calls at great financial sacrifice for both of us. F— took his second plane trip, this time three thousand miles to see me in Trinidad. Then it all ended abruptly, without warning it seemed to me, though when I look back I should have seen the proverbial writing on the wall. F— had begun to tell me about a girl he met who knew all about me because he had told her all about me. She even shared my first name, with, I eventually saw in hindsight, a formidable distinction. One letter in her name was different from mine and it set her apart from me, not only in nationality and ethnicity, but also in the hierarchy of America's social class. She was a New England Brahmin, irresistible to F— who had ambitions to climb to the top of New York society. She could open doors for him; I would be a liability. His letter breaking up with me was loaded with metaphors that I supposed assuaged his Catholic guilt. She was the rock; I was the waves crashing against the shore, whatever that meant. Decades later and divorced by then, F— would show me the manuscript of a novel he was writing about a brilliant white lawyer who discovers he was denied partner in a WASP law firm because he was married to a beautiful black Jamaican woman. Incensed, the man goes on a killing spree in revenge. Well, I thought, at least the woman was beautiful!

I was heartbroken when F— got engaged to his New England Brahmin, but I did not change my plans. I headed to New York. I enrolled in graduate school and worked during the day to pay for classes I took at night. I covered up my hurt with the veneer of New York sophistication.

Mary did not understand. All she knew was that I was unreachable in some unexplainable way. We continued to be close, but we did not pry under the shell we had both built around ourselves, I with a sort of wild gaiety, she with a dark and forbidding silence.

We are in a good place now, Mary and I, good friends, loyal sisters. Still, she keeps me tethered to a rope, parceling out information in small increments when and how she wants. I no longer play her game. Which was why I did not question her further when she first told me she was going on a cruise to Alaska. Which is why I forgot the name of the ocean liner though she had given it to me in her phone message.

Luckily, we have a sister-in-law, Beverly, who was once in the travel agency business. Beverly will track down Mary for us, Jacqueline assures me.

When Jacqueline leaves with Judith to meet Beverly, who is staying with Karen, I tiptoe down the corridor to my parents' bedroom to check on my father. I do not want to disturb him but I need to know if he has finally been able to rest. I press my ear to the door. I hear movement, footsteps going back and forth from one side of the room to the other. Alarmed, I knock on the door. The voice that tells me to come in is calm, not at all agitated, as I feared. I enter the room. My father is in his pajamas, a checkered navy and light blue ensemble, long-sleeved jacket, long pants. My mother liked to sleep with the air conditioner turned to its coldest and my father, adjusting his nighttime wardrobe to suit her wishes, wears flannel pajamas to bed. He stands silently in front of me, his hands piled high with the comforter. For years it has been his job in the evening to take the comforter out of the closet, where my mother puts it every morning, and lay it on the bed for the night. "Do you want me to help you?" I ask. He shakes his head and, without a word, turns away. I watch in silence as he stretches the comforter across the side of the bed where my mother slept, and across the side of the bed where he sleeps. He takes his time walking around the bed from one side to the other, back and forth, smoothing the comforter with the palm of his hand so that it lies down flat. He does not turn it down as he usually does.

Soon he picks up the two pillows on his side of the
bed and places them in a vertical line, one behind the
other. *What is he doing?* I dare not ask. He reaches for the
other two pillows on my mother's side and places them
behind the first set of pillows. The line of pillows extends
from the top of the bed to the bottom. He still has not
spoken, but now he straightens up and acknowledges
my presence. He smiles. There is no joy in his smile. It's
a sort of sly smile that a child would give when caught
doing something he should not do yet hoping to be par-
doned. There is no light in my father's eyes though, no
mischievous twinkle. They are profoundly sad, so sad
that I cannot bear to face him. I twist my head around,
away from him.

"I know what I am doing," my father says, as if he
has taken my reaction as a criticism, a chastisement.

"And what is that, Daddy?" I ask, turning back to him.

He does not reply. He fluffs the pillows and smiles
that sad smile again. Then it strikes me that what he is
doing is building a barrier between his side of the bed
and his wife's. *He has finally accepted her death. He has accepted
that she will not be coming back, that he must ready himself for
nights without her.* I feel tears welling in my eyes. I need to
leave before he sees them fall. "I'm going to make some
tea," I say. "Would you like some?"

He nods.

Jacqueline and Judith have not come back. It is still
early—six o'clock—but the house is dark. My parents
live in a valley and when the sun goes down behind the
mountain range that faces the house, night descends
quickly. All is quiet, just the sounds of the leaves swish-

ing against each other in the slight breeze. The birds are asleep, roosting in the trees. Suddenly in the distance I hear the hooting of an owl. It is the bird that is said to embody the spirit, the haunting messenger that connects the living to the dead.

Not long after I arrived at my parents' home, Karen called. She told me that after she left the hospital where my mother had just died, an owl accompanied her to her home. She was driving, she said, and her son was next to her in the passenger seat. Her cell phone rang and the caller ID popped up. *Mummy*, it announced. But when her son pressed the talk button, no one was on the phone. Then they saw the owl. It flew next to them and never left their side until Karen pulled into her garage.

Do I believe her story? The owl I hear now hooting in the distance erases my instinct to be skeptical. *Where are you, Mummy?* The darkness and the call of the owl intensify my grief. I feel utterly alone. I wish my sisters were here. I need someone to comfort me, someone to help me comfort my father. I must be strong. I cannot indulge my needs. Not now. My father has lost his wife. He needs me. I hear the flutter of wings again, then silence. The owl has gone.

I return to my parents' room with tea for my father. He is lying curled up, facing the side of the bed where my mother sleeps. One arm is under the pillow that is at the top of the line of pillows he has placed along the bed, the other arm over it. His legs are intertwined around the pillows at the bottom.

The pillows are *her*, the body he has embraced for sixty-five years. How stupid I have been! How little I have understood him! How little I know of enduring love! He was not building a barrier *against* my mother. He wanted to get closer to her. He was hugging her.

I put down the cup on his bedside table. My fingers are shaking when I touch his shoulder. "I brought you tea, Daddy." He does not move. He does not utter a sound. For he does not want tea. What he wants is to hold his wife. I withdraw my hand. "I'll stay here until you fall asleep," I say. He tightens his arms and legs around the pillows and draws his body closer to my mother's side of the bed.

The owl returns. It hoots softly this time, a melody it seems to me that ripples through the room. My father opens his eyes and smiles. The owl hoots for a last time and flies away, its wings grazing the window. My father closes his eyes. In seconds he's asleep.

The night gets deeper. I sit down on the armchair next to my father's side of the bed. Soon I am asleep too. When Jacqueline calls my name, I am startled.

8

J acqueline used to be a bank manager. She had the reputation of running the most efficient of her bank's branches. She has taken charge of the funeral arrangements with the same efficiency and urgency. Now she has come to order me into action. "Wake up, Elizabeth!" She tugs my arm.

I put my finger to my lips and incline my head toward my father who is breathing evenly on the bed. "Shush," I whisper. But my father has not stirred. His sleep is so deep he does not hear when Jacqueline calls me again.

"Come, Elizabeth!" She raises her voice and beckons me out my parents' room. "We have to select a dress for Mummy."

I get up from the armchair but I do not want to follow her. For years I have bought my mother's clothes. Whatever dress we select for her will surely be one I had chosen for her from the racks of the department stores in Long Island where I usually bought her clothes.

Jacqueline notices my hesitation. "You have to come now." Her voice is stern. She will brook no objections from me. "The funeral parlor needs the dress tonight. *Tonight*, Elizabeth."

I think I bought my mother her first ready-made dress. I had asked her for her measurements, and with the help of a saleslady at Macy's, I figured out she was size 14 and bought her a beautiful royal-blue linen Jones New York dress. It fit her perfectly. With her exquisite sense of fashion, she wore it with a string of white pearls over the thin gold chain with the gold crucifix pendant she never took off. The effect was an aristocratic elegance. But then my mother, even in the years when my father's salary was barely enough to feed, clothe, and shelter us, always managed to look like an aristocrat.

When Yolande, Jacqueline, Mary, and I were children, my mother used to sew our clothes on an old foot-pedal Singer sewing machine. The stores in Trinidad did not yet sell ready-made clothes—but even if they did, my parents could not afford to buy them, not with eight children at that time, four girls and four boys. We could always measure our mother's anger by the furious drumbeat of the iron pedal on the sewing machine slamming back and forth against the wood floor, and the sounds of fabric ripping and tearing with the mistakes she often made. We knew to stay far away from her at those times. My brother Gregory was not easily intimidated, however. He was a mischievous boy and loved playing tricks on our mother. He once called her from a pay phone and, imitating a thick American accent, told her that she had been selected to win a new refrigerator. Before she could get her prize, however, she had to answer four questions. "Who discovered Trinidad?" That was his first question, and, of course, my mother knew the answer. "Christopher Columbus," she said. This was in the days before people began voicing their indignation that an island already populated with people could be said to be "discovered." My brother went on: "What is the capital of Trinidad?" "Port of Spain," my mother answered excitedly. "Name the two bodies of water on the west and east coasts of Trinidad." My mother was on a roll: "The Gulf of Paria on the west, and the Atlantic on the east." "Now, madam," my brother continued, measuring out his words in long syllables, perfectly imitating the guttural rolling sounds we heard from the Yankees who lived on the military base on our island, "here comes the last question. It's a hard one, madam, but if you can answer it . . ." My mother began shooing the rest of us to be quiet. "Here is the question, madam. Why did Columbus give our island the name Trinidad?" At that point my mother was jumping for joy. She knew that answer too, as did every schoolchild in Trinidad. "He named it for the Holy Trinity when he saw the three mountain ranges in Trinidad—the northern range, the central range, and the southern range." My brother let out a loud whoop. "Tonight, madam, you will get your prize. A shining new refrigerator will be delivered to your home. Look out for it!"

Night fell and the skies darkened and yet the promised refrigerator did not arrive. My mother had told all her neighbors about the contest she had won; she had cleaned out a space in the kitchen for her grand prize. At last, taking pity on her, my brother confessed. My mother's punishment for him, as for all the tricks he continued to play on her, was to have him kneel on the floor next to her while she was sewing. With each mistake she made, she would take out her frustration on poor Gregory. *Whack!* We would hear the sound of her hand on his bottom.

My sister Karen does not like to revisit tales of the days when our mother could not afford to hire a seamstress to sew our clothes or the times when butter was a luxury for us, or when we had to cut a hole at the tip of our watchicongs, the canvas shoes we wore, to fit our growing feet, or when at Christmastime our mother finally threw out our pee-soaked mattresses and had the local tailor sew new ones for us out of canvas sheeting he filled with fibers from dried coconut husks, or when she raised chickens and turkeys to sell to our neighbors. Karen thinks somehow these tales are part of my imaginings, a fiction I tell to unsettle her romantic notions of our parents' rise up the ladder of Trinidad's high society.

Of all my sisters, Karen was closest to my mother. She is as tall as my mother was and has her same broad, shapely hips and narrow waist, but she does not so much resemble my mother as she shares her sense of social decorum and her fierce vigilance of the closet where our family's skeletons were firmly locked. But I remember those days well when money was scarce for our family. I remember the sickening smell of chicken excrement in the drawing room and the peck, pecking of the baby chicks, like the tapping of a Morse code, echoing throughout the house.

Karen is not to be blamed, however. She can have no memory of those days. By the time she was four, the ninth of my parents' eleven children, our fortunes had changed dramatically. My father had accepted a managerial position with the Shell Oil Company and money was no longer the constant problem it had been for us. But before then, before the days when having chicken for dinner was a luxury our parents could barely afford— and then, just once a week on Sundays—my mother turned our drawing room into a nursery for baby chicks and baby turkeys. The morris chairs were pushed to one side to make room for rows of wire cages on wood stilts, where my mother put the baby chicks and turkeys when they were hatched. She lined the cages with newspaper, and it was my job to remove the excrement-filled newspaper and replace it with clean sheets. I date my revulsion for callaloo from the day I was assigned that chore.

Callaloo is Trinidad's national dish. Every red-blooded Trinidadian loves callaloo—callaloo with crabs, callaloo with pig tails, callaloo with coconut milk. The main ingredients are the broad dark green leaves of the dasheen plant and okra, both boiled to a pulp. The effect is a dish that to me looks not unlike the droppings of chickens: green and slimy. Had I not already thought so, my brother David, fifteen months my junior and the bane of my existence when we were children, would have pointed out the similarity to me, as he did one day when we were having our big Sunday lunch where callaloo featured prominently. He turned to me with his spoon dripping with callaloo—slimy, green, dotted with okra seeds like the tiny pieces of grain the chickens had consumed—and smiling wickedly, he addressed me by my nickname, which to this day he still calls me: "Betty, look. Chicken crap." He slurped the slime down his throat.

My brothers were responsible for slaughtering the chickens and turkeys my mother sold. Slaughtering poultry then was not clean, sanitized work. My bothers would lay the poor things on a slab of wood or stone, pull them by their heads until their necks were stretched taut, and then slice the heads off with a machete. Blood would splatter everywhere. Sometimes the poor things would not realize their heads were cut off and would run in circles, each the proverbial chicken without a head.

I would be revolted, but David seemed inured to all that blood. He would become a skilled surgeon years later. My older sister Yolande, who became a midwife and later often supervised nurses in the surgery unit, told me that residents flocked to the OR when my brother was operating on a patient. They said he was the best OB-GYN surgeon in all of New Jersey.

My mother sold eggs as well as poultry. Still, the money she made to supplement my father's salary was not enough to feed us. So my father's hobby became a necessity for us. We depended on the game and fish he caught when he went hunting or fishing with his friends on the weekends. My mother was always generous. She would share my father's catch with our neighbors who, like her, had many mouths to feed. In the weeks after my father returned from his fishing expeditions or from the hunt, we ate like royalty. It wasn't until I was in my early twenties that I discovered that the wild meat we had eaten could have killed us. At the World's Fair in New York I was attracted to an exhibit that boasted the largest rat in the world. The largest rat in the world turned out to be an agouti. My father hunted agouti. I had eaten it stewed, I had eaten it curried, I think I had even eaten it barbecued.

I don't know if it was around the time of my father's fishing and hunting days that my mother began wearing the gold chain with the gold cross pendant she never took off, whether she was in her day clothes at home or going to the fanciest party. Perhaps it was that time. I know she always lived in fear of something happening to my father, either in the rainforests in the interior of the island or on the rough seas. Both were dangerous. Our Amazonian forest, cut off from the South American continent in an ancient seismic shift, was darkened by thick looping vines that entwined themselves up tall trees and was crowded with all sorts of wild animals and long, undulating snakes. Our seas to the north and south of the west coast were cemeteries of pirates' ships, no match for the roiling currents.

Once, when he was hunting in the forest, my father stepped on a macajuel snake he thought was a thick log. "Was it huge like a boa constrictor?" I asked. I was ten years old and already a voracious reader. I knew about the boa constrictor in Saint-Exupéry's *The Little Prince*. It had eaten an elephant. "Could a macajuel snake eat an elephant?" My father humored me. "Yes, if it was hungry." And in fact it could—a baby elephant—for macajuel was our name for the boa constrictor, many of them stranded on the part of the Amazon that formed our island.

I had nightmares for weeks after my father had barely escaped being swallowed whole by a macajuel snake and never protested when my mother called us to pray for him, a rosary every night, five o'clock Mass on Saturdays, and nine o'clock Mass on Sundays. And when my father returned, more prayers to express our gratitude to God. Of course, little did I know that even after my father returned from hunting, he was still in danger, and all of us too, even more so. *Bush meat* is how the meat my father brought home is referred to today. It can be the source of all sorts of insidious viruses. We were lucky.

None of us fell ill from touching or eating the flesh of the wild animals my father hunted.

I loved that chain with the gold cross my mother began wearing around her neck when my father went hunting in the forest, and had visions of owning it one day. As I follow Jacqueline now to the room where my mother stored her better dresses, I wonder if my siblings will insist that we bury her with the gold chain. I want the gold chain, I feel I deserve it, but all these thoughts leave me when Jacqueline reaches into the closet and pulls out a rose-pink dress. I had bought that dress for my mother. The tags are still on it. I had given it to her two months ago. The fabric is soft, flirty. In spite of many pregnancies that had broadened her hips, my mother had a relatively small, well-defined waistline. I had imagined the top of the dress draping down to her belted waist. I had imagined the skirt falling smoothly from her hips and fluttering around her legs.

"This will look good on Mummy," Jacqueline announces.

The dress is to become our mother's shroud, and one of my sisters will claim the gold chain with the crucifix.

9

I wake up early the next morning to the sound of
dishes crashing onto the hard surface of the terrazzo-
tiled kitchen floor. My eyes skid to the clock on
the bureau in the bedroom. Five ten. It was past eleven
when Jacqueline left, taking the dress for our mother
with her. When I checked on my father, he was still in
a deep sleep, curled up on the bed, still hugging the pillows. I shut the door quietly behind me and went to the
girls' room.

We call the bedroom where I slept the girls' room
though it has been years—eons, it seems—since either
I or any of my five sisters have been girls. There is also
a boys' room where some of my brothers, two of them
already grandfathers, stay when they visit our parents.
I stumble out of bed, shaken roughly from my sleep by
the clatter in the kitchen. The sun is beginning to rise,
but there is not enough light outside my window to distinguish the colors of the fruit trees and flowers in the
garden. All are dark silhouettes against the shimmering
dark-blue sky. It is too early for Petra to have arrived, so
the noise I heard in the kitchen can mean only one thing:
my father is awake.

He apologizes as soon as he sees me. "I dropped the
cup," he says. "I didn't intend to wake you." I help him
pick up the shards scattered across the floor. His hands

are shaking slightly. I avert my eyes. When we have swept up the fragments, he offers to make a cup of coffee for me. I tell him I only drink tea. He shakes his head. "Coffee keeps you alert," he says.

He wants to be alert. He wants to be in full control of his senses when he sees his wife.

"It's too early." I do not have to say more. He knows what I mean.

"Oh, we can go after breakfast," he says. "I was just making coffee."

He makes coffee every morning for my mother and takes it to her in their bedroom. I notice he has removed only one cup and one saucer from the cupboard. I take this as another sign he has accepted that my mother will not be coming home, will never be coming home.

"I'll call again," I say. "I'll find out what time we can go." *To the funeral parlor*, I could have added, but I do not. My father's eyes warn me to say no more. He knows *to the funeral parlor*. His cup rattles against the saucer when he shuffles back to his room.

When did my father begin his gradual decline? He had retired early from the Shell Oil Company, when he was only fifty-seven. Our island had gained its independence from Britain, and the oilmen from England, Holland, and America who owned the company had begun divesting their holdings, aware that it would only be a matter of time before the island would take control of its natural resources. They gave my father a generous severance package, but he continued to work as a labor consultant for decades afterward, representing private and public interests in the Industrial Court in Trinidad and at the

International Labour Organization in Geneva, where he was already well known during his years working for both the colonial government and Shell. Then one day he was putting butter in his tea. I was there to see him do it.

We were having breakfast and I asked him if he wanted more sugar. "I'll get it," he said, and stuck his spoon in the butter dish.

I reached to help him but my mother stopped me. "He just wants your attention," she said angrily. "He knows perfectly well what he is doing."

Did he?

Ten years ago I made the trip to Columbus, Mississippi, to see my parents. They were visiting my brother Gregory and his wife Beverly. My mother had passed the five-year threshold for breast cancer survivors, and she wanted to travel again. She chose to visit Gregory, I think not only because he is a doctor, and she felt more comfortable being in his home in case her illness flared up again, but also because she had a soft spot for this son of hers who had endured the blows she had rained on his bottom and legs. No longer in constant fear that my father's paltry salary from the colonial government, together with the little money she managed to eke out from her domestic poultry farm, would be enough to feed her ever-expanding brood, my mother became more relaxed as she grew older. At the same time, however, she was tortured by guilt that she had been too hard on us, especially on Gregory. I think especially Gregory because, unlike the rest of us, he never got angry with her, he never pouted; he never gave her the silent treatment for days, my specialty.

Gregory took his blows without rancor but he continued to play tricks on my mother. After the ruse of the fake contest for a new refrigerator, there were others. My mother was always fooled. She never seemed able to detect Gregory's voice under the foreign accents he used, but in her defense I would say that my brother was a master of vocal disguise. He also made her laugh, particularly when she got frustrated with the mistakes she constantly made trying to sew dresses for my sisters and me. Somehow she rarely seemed able to fit sleeves in the armholes she had cut out from the fabric; either she made them too big or too small. Gregory would help her out of her predicament. "Rip them out, Mum, rip them out," he would say, joining forces with her. "Your machine telling you it too hot for sleeves." My mother would burst out laughing and together they would start pulling seams apart. Pieces of cloth would go flying into the air.

My parents seemed happy when I saw them in the bucolic setting of Gregory's home in Mississippi. The tall leafy trees, the green grass, the gently undulating hills, the intermittent whistle of birds as they glided through the warm, turgid air must have reminded them of tropical Trinidad. The first morning I was there my father wanted me to go walking with him. He wanted to show me the birds he had identified in the woods on either side of the road that sloped gently down from my brother's home and then steeply up before descending again. I trailed behind my father, huffing and puffing with every ascent. Even at eighty-three my father was a brisk walker. He could climb to the top of a hill without pausing for breath.

The year before, my father had driven me up the winding road to the Asa Wright bird sanctuary in the dense rainforest of the northern mountain range in Trinidad. The area, once known as the Spring Hill Estate, used to be a thriving cocoa plantation, but the cocoa industry had dried up when oil was discovered in the south of the island. Asa and Newcombe Wright, the owners of Spring Hill, turned the estate into a sanctuary for wildlife. It became particularly well known for the rare birds that nested in the forest trees. At one point 159 species of birds were recorded there. My father loved going to Asa Wright. The day I went with him he shamed me and a group of bird lovers, some half his age, by trotting up the inclines while most of us had to take breaks to catch our breath. I discovered my father had gone to the bird sanctuary so many times the workers there knew him well enough to address him by name. We had lunch in the dining room and the cook came out of the kitchen to greet him. "Red beans and rice again, Mr. Nunez?" the man asked. As far as I could see there were no red beans and rice on the cafeteria-style counter, but stewed red beans and rice are what my father had for lunch.

My father loved birds, his interest ignited by his forest warden father who was himself influenced by his Portuguese father who had chosen to work on the cocoa plantation rather than follow his Portuguese compatriots into the dry-goods business. So intimate was my father's relationship with the birds in Trinidad, he could call out to them in their distinctive whistles and they would respond in kind. In the early days, my father used this skill to trap the birds. He would whistle to them, luring them to the branch of a tree he had lined with laglee, a gluey substance. When the birds alighted on the branch, they would get stuck and my father would pluck them out and cage them. I had grown up with birdcages dangling from wires attached to the ceiling of our porch. Then, surprisingly, when I returned home from college, the cages were no longer there. My father had set the birds free. He did the same with his fish, though the empty tank still remained where it was, a reminder I presume he wanted of the thoughtlessness of his youth. The disappearance of those cages and that empty fish tank would be a lesson to me. Though my father did not give me an explanation for what he had done, his unspoken message was clear: we had no right to take a living creature out of its natural habitat just to serve our pleasure.

In those days, as now, my father's joy came from looking and "talking" to the birds, he in his habitat, they in theirs. All along that country road in Columbus, Mississippi, my father whistled to the American birds, as he had done with the birds in Trinidad, and they whistled back to him. My father seemed vigorous and alert, in full control of his enormous intellect. I was certain my mother was right. The butter in the tea was my father's call for attention. Nothing was wrong with his brain. Confident that he had been simply toying with me, I decided to seek his help with a problem that had been troubling me. Gregory was a chain-smoker. Nothing I said or did seemed to convince him that he should stop smoking, not my alarm at his constant dry cough, nor the statistics I recited to him on lung cancer and heart disease.

"Gregory's house is practically blue with smoke," I complained to my father.

I had said the same to my brother and he countered, "When we were children, our house was always blue with smoke and we survived."

It was true. We had survived, and all of us apparently in good health. My father was a chain-smoker too. For sixteen years growing up in my parents' home, I rarely saw my father without a cigarette. We lived in the tropics, so our windows were always open, yet our house was suffused with the stink of cigarettes; it was embedded in the furniture and in our clothes. Cigarette ashes were piled up everywhere in saucers and ashtrays. I still remember the colorful plastic ashtrays I bought for my father for Christmas and his birthday. They were the best gifts I could think of giving him.

"Dad is eighty-three," Gregory reminded me. "Statistics don't tell the truth for everyone."

But our father did not wake up every morning with a racking cough.

Now, as we climbed the incline toward Gregory's house, I pleaded with my father to speak to him. My father slowed down and faced me. "I am to blame," he said softly. "I set a bad example."

I tried to convince him he was wrong. "But you stopped. Gregory could have learned that from you too."

"Gregory was already a man when I stopped," he replied.

This was not accurate. Gregory was not yet a man when my father stopped smoking. He was fourteen, still a child, when he first began pilfering my father's cigarettes. The ones he stole from my father were not the filtered type; those had not yet reached our island. There was no wad at the bottom to dilute some of the poisons that would course through the smoker's lungs. The cigarettes my father inhaled, sucking the dark smoke deep into his lungs, were unfiltered. I know because I bought cartons of unfiltered cigarettes for him in the duty-free shops every time I returned to Trinidad on holiday.

My father stopped smoking in his mid-fifties, abruptly and without forethought, though he would say that he had tried to stop years before then. He was on the sea this time, in an open pirogue with his godson, a young man in his early teens. They were out fishing. The sun was beating down on their heads, and my father, perhaps to ease the sting of the sun burning his flesh, sought comfort in the familiar pleasure of smoking. He dug into his pocket, took out a cigarette, and lit it. According to his version of the story, his godson turned to him and made this innocent request: "Uncle, why you don't throw that cigarette in the sea?" And that is exactly what my father did. He threw the lit cigarette into the sea and never touched another one again.

"It is the one major regret in my life," my father said to me as I quickened my pace to catch up with him. "I taught my sons to smoke."

I reminded him that his sons were men now. If Gregory wanted, he could get help to break the habit.

My father shook his head sadly. "I would be the happiest person in the world if Gregory would quit. He is such a good son to me."

I did not see then that my father's eyes had become misty, or notice, as we approached the house, that the jauntiness had gone out of his stride. I was too distracted by the presence of my brother's car in the driveway, thrilled that he had come home for lunch. If my father had set a bad example for his sons with his cigarette habit, he had set a good one as a man who put his family before his ambitions, for I had no doubt that Gregory had to reschedule his patients' appointments to be here with us in time for lunch.

My father did not have patients, of course, but he was an ambitious young man, a junior officer at the Ministry of Labour, with his eye on the top of the ladder, a not unfounded possibility for a non-European in the days just before independence, and yet he risked that ambition to have lunch with his children almost every day when we were in school.

My father eventually made it to the top of the ladder. He was in his early forties when he was appointed commissioner of labor. The previous commissioner, Solomon Hochoy, was the first nonwhite British governor of Trinidad and Tobago. Later, when our island gained independence, he was made governor general and knighted by the Queen of England. Though Sir Solomon had not achieved this status when my father worked in the ministry, the signs were already there that he was favored by the British. It was also likely that if any local man was to rise in the British colonial government, it would be someone attached to the Ministry of Labour, which was the first of the ministries the British colonial government had more or less entrusted to locals. Two world wars, the failing sugarcane economy, and the persistent drumbeat for decolonization across the globe had made the British skittish. If problems came, they would come from the labor force. Better to have one of the people's own in charge of the labor ministry when the onslaught rumbled through the island.

So it was not at all far-fetched for us to assume that our father's future looked very bright indeed. Yet every day my father left his office at lunchtime to pick us up from school. I was at Tranquility Girls School then, the equivalent of American middle school. Yolande and Richard were in high school, she at the prestigious St. Joseph's Convent for girls, and he on scholarship at the equally prestigious St. Mary's College for boys. David and Jacqueline were in elementary school. At around noon, soon after my school broke for lunch, I would see my father turning the corner in his sky-blue Rambler, one of the perks of his position as commissioner of labor. He would already have picked up Yolande and Richard, and after getting me, he would go for David and Jacqueline. How he managed to do this, I have no idea. I cannot imagine that all his affairs at the ministry ended just before noon, or that a meeting with a superior would be conveniently scheduled to allow him to go home at exactly that time. It must have been risky for him to leave his office, and yet he rarely failed. Sometimes he was late, but always I knew the Rambler would be turning the corner and soon I would be having lunch with him, my mother, and my siblings.

Family comes first, my father said. And so Gregory was following in his father's footsteps. He would drop everything, reschedule his patients' appointments, and have lunch with his mother and father.

The house was thrumming with happy voices when we came into the dining room. My sister-in-law Beverly, who is Jamaican, had made pelau for lunch. Pelau is a quintessential Trinidadian dish which locals contend only they know how to make properly. My mother had apparently just complimented Beverly on the tenderness of the chicken and the graininess of the rice, and Gregory, who was sitting at the head of the table, was grinning from ear to ear with pride. Next to his hand was a lit cigarette resting on an ashtray, already burned halfway down and sending a thin trail of smoke across the table. As he got up to greet our father, Gregory reached for the cigarette and was about to put it to his lips when I pounced on him. "Do you know how miserable you are making Daddy?" I yelled. "He said the greatest regret in his life is that you are still smoking. My God, don't you care about him?" More accusations flew out of my mouth like venom.

My father sat down heavily in his chair. "I am to blame," he murmured. And for the first time I noticed the moisture in his eyes.

Gregory put down his cigarette, threw me a scathing look, and then turned his back on me. "So, Dad," he began as if I had not said a word to him, "how was your day? Catch any birds? Picoplat? Chikechong?" He smiled at my father adoringly.

In an instant my father's mood changed. "I saw one today," he chirped. His face brightened.

"A picoplat?"

"No, a semp. A really nice one. Bright yellow feathers on his breast. Black streaks too."

"And the wings?"

"White. The brightest white you ever saw."

"Did you whistle to him?"

"Yes. And he whistled back."

I simmered with indignation. There were no picoplats, chikechongs, or semps in Mississippi. Those were tropical birds. But I stifled my anger. My father looked too happy, and I was loathe to extinguish the light shining with increasing brightness in his eyes.

Back and forth my brother and father went talking about semps, picoplats, and chikechongs, about which had the brightest feathers, which made the sweetest music. Then suddenly my father turned to me. "You saw the semp too, didn't you, Elizabeth?"

What could I say? Could I deny him the joy of remembering his days in the forest singing with the birds? Before I could think up an answer, he began to whistle, an exact imitation of the song of the yellow-feathered semp. I didn't know what to do, what to say. I gestured to my brother for help. He whistled back as if he were a semp too, and for a while he and my father continued this way, with call and response, until abruptly my father stopped waiting for my brother's response. Now his whistles became shriller, louder, more frantic.

"Dad." My brother moved closer to him. I could tell he was getting nervous. "Dad."

My father continued to whistle.

"Dad!"

My father pursed his lips to whistle again, but this time no sound came out of his mouth. "It's my fault," he murmured. He hung down his head. "I'm to blame. My fault."

My mother placed her hand on his arm. "Come, Waldo." She tugged his arm gently.

My father glanced over at her.

"Waldo," my mother crooned. "Come now. Let's go. It's time for a nap."

So she knew. So my mother was aware that my father

was drifting away. Her anger with me when I tried to still his hand as he reached for the butter to put in his tea was really her terror, her fear that she could be losing her partner in life, the man who had traveled with her through all the sorrows, joys, failures, and triumphs of their more than sixty years together. She had said my father made a conscious decision to give up. He would not allow himself to be taken by surprise; he would be ready when the Grim Reaper came. My father was pretending to be weak, she said, shuffling back and forth through the house like a senile old man, but I know now she was the one pretending, hoping against hope she was right.

My father wanted my attention, but he did not know what he was doing, not when he reached for the butter to put in his tea, not when he began unraveling a tale about seeing picoplats, chikechongs, and semps in the forest near my brother's house in Mississippi, not when my brother led him down this path and he could not find his way back to what troubled him so deeply: he was to blame for my brother's nicotine habit.

My brother did not spare me from his fury when he returned from the bedroom where he and my mother had talked my father into taking an afternoon nap. "See what you've done!" He waved his finger at me. "You've put bad thoughts in Dad's head. You! *You* have done that! Dad needs to be peaceful. He needs to have happy thoughts. You have upset him."

How am I to give my father happy thoughts now when his wife has just died? How can I give him peace?

I call the funeral parlor. As a special favor to the family, the receptionist tells me, the owner has agreed to arrange a showing for my father. *A showing*, she says, as if my mother is already an artifact in a museum. "We can't have all of you," she informs me. She knows we are eleven, and with our spouses, partners, and children, we make up a crowd. "Just you and your father."

Just me and my father. I do not know if I can hold up with just me and my father. If I can be strong enough for him.

10

My three doctor brothers say that our father does not have Alzheimer's. If he had Alzheimer's he would not recognize us. And there is no denying that ten years after I watched in increasing alarm as past and present got mangled in my father's head, he has not entirely lost contact with reality. He knows who we are, all eleven of us. He addresses us by name. More amazingly, for it's a feat that stumps me, my father recognizes our voices even when he cannot see us. It takes him just a heartbeat to know who I am when I call from New York. "Elizabeth! How are you, Elizabeth?" he warbles happily.

Gregory informs me that Alzheimer's is one of the diseases associated with dementia, the most extreme, he says. Our father is on the low end of the dementia scale. He knows who he is, he knows where he lives, he can take care of his bodily functions without assistance. Skills of a four-year-old, I think when Gregory produces this evidence of our father's mental acuity. I remain unconvinced. Impaired acuity, I say to myself. By any name, my father's decline has been precipitous.

My uncle John says that my father has simply chosen to withdraw into himself, a position my mother often articulated, though I know now she did so out of fear. According to my uncle, the two most brilliant of my grandparents' nine children were my uncle George and my father. When George was killed, my father inherited the mantle alone, without competition from his other siblings. "He is a genius," my uncle concedes, and then adds with what I detect is a hint of bitterness in his voice, "or *was*."

Uncle George was killed flying a British bomber over Germany. He was one of hundreds of young men from Trinidad and Tobago who volunteered to fight for the British in World War II. Loyalty to the Crown was not their primary motive. Ulric Cross, a mathematician, who later became a sought-after lawyer and respected judge, told me that he and his friends volunteered when Pope Pius XII gave his blessing to Mussolini to kill Africans in Ethiopia. The men from T&T were fighting with the British, Ulric explained, but their real reason for joining the war was to avenge the slaughter of Africans. Most of the men from our twin islands wanted to be in the Royal Air Force, either as pilots, navigators, or bombardiers, but only an elite few were chosen. They were the ones who excelled in mathematics and science. Uncle George was one of the 252 men who were chosen. On one of his missions, his plane was shot down.

"If you ask me," my uncle John says, "pride is your father's downfall. He didn't suffer fools gladly, and when he was no longer as quick on his feet as he used to be, he decided to withdraw rather than have people see he was losing his memory and his prized cognitive skills. But age does that. We all lose some memory as we get older. We all are no longer as quick with answers as we used to be. But pride—pride got the better of your father."

My youngest brother Roger once made the same

observation to me: "Dad can't stand that now he can't come up with answers as fast as he once did. So he has the brain of a fifty-year-old! So what? He's in his eighties, for God's sake! But he'd rather pretend he can't hear, or he's disinterested, than for someone to find out he's lost his edge."

Perhaps that was so. But as my father slid deeper into his eighties, it became more and more apparent that something was radically wrong. He would enter a discussion energetically, his points lucid and coherent, but soon his mind would wander and he would lose the thread. One afternoon, two of my friends from the States, university scholars who had come with me to Trinidad to attend a conference at the University of the West Indies in St. Augustine, dropped by my parents' home. They got very excited when they learned of my father's history, particularly his involvement in the oil industry before and after colonialism. My father got very excited too. He was once again the center of attention, on that platform he had held for many years as a labor negotiator representing the colonial government, and, later, the oil industry, and then finally, when he retired from Shell, as a consultant for the labor unions and big business.

As the two academics crowded around him, my father began sensibly enough, arms swinging in the air as he emphasized this point and that, and then I heard the familiar guffaw. "Those boys from Venezuela . . . went fishing." A memory of something from the distant past had found its way through a slit in his brain. His eyes danced mischievously, hoarse laughter rumbled up his throat. He snorted trying to hold it back. "Well, my friends and I taught those boys a thing or two," he said, grinning wickedly.

"Which boys? Who was with you?" My friends had been taking notes and were earnestly trying to make sense of my father's detour.

"Butler, he . . ." my father continued.

"Uriah Butler?"

"Yes, Uriah. He was on the pirogue too. Think we didn't know where the border ends? Can't see it under the water, but I know which part of the oil is theirs and which is ours."

Uriah Butler was a trade unionist who led the 1937 oil field workers strike in Trinidad. In 1937, my father was twenty-three, working as an assistant to a chemist in the oil fields. He never went fishing with Butler, but he often went with his own friends.

I pulled my colleagues aside. "My father is tired," I said.

My explanation may have satisfied them; it did not satisfy Jacqueline. As our father kept drifting further and further away from us she became angry with him. "I depended on him," she later grumbled to me. "I used to be able to take all my problems at work to him and he'd help me out. Now he just pushes me away."

I empathized with her frustration. Our parents' bedroom was the center of our world. Even when we were in our forties and fifties, we would gather there, my siblings who were still on the island dropping by on their way home from work, the ones living abroad making my parents' home their first and last stop on their way to and from the airport. No matter where we found our father, in the garden or doing some minor chore for our mother, we always managed to steer him to the bedroom he shared with her.

There, seated on the edge of his bed (for one of us would always take his bedside armchair), my father would listen attentively and patiently as we spilled out our problems. His advice was always sensible. He was quick to separate facts from the guises we used, intentionally or not, to avoid facing the truth. His yardstick was always a strict adherence to ethical principles and compassion for the underdog. "When I put my head down on my pillow at night," he used to say to us, "I want to know I have not intentionally hurt anyone." But when my sisters and I brought our difficulties with our spouses to him, he would shake his head and a pained expression would enter his eyes. He would do anything for us, he would say, but he could not help us with our marital problems. He had a standing position against interfering in his children's marriages. "You can never tell what goes on between a husband and wife behind closed doors." Still, he would offer us consolation: "The longest rope has an end." Or he'd say, "You'll sort it out. You'll see." Platitudes, but from him, words to live by.

My mother generally stayed silent during these talks, occasionally nodding her head in agreement or smiling encouragingly. She was in awe of her husband, and believed, as we did, that he was a genius. On every important matter, she deferred to him. Or at least this is how it seemed to us. We were adults, with our own families, before we realized that our father made no decision without our mother's approval. But my mother belonged to a generation of women who wanted their men to seem manly, or perhaps it was that they *needed* their men to feel manly. The man, after all, was often the sole breadwinner. They depended on him for their survival and the survival of their children.

Strangely, though, as our father began to decline, our mother started to shine, and we found out, happily not too late, that she too was brilliant.

Quite accidentally I discovered that she read books. I didn't think she did. I thought her only interests were domestic, all related to her children, her home, and her social circles. It turned out, however, that she had read my first novel, *When Rocks Dance*. I hadn't expected her to. Years ago I had left the novel for my father. He never read it. As far as I know, he never read a single one of my eight books. When I found out my mother had read *When Rocks Dance*, I gave her my next two novels, *Beyond the Limbo Silence* and *Bruised Hibiscus*. She read them too and was full of praise for me. I was her favorite author, she said.

As the past and the present became more and more indistinguishable to my father, my mother continued to blossom. Soon I was sending her the manuscripts of novels I was working on. She became my most enthusiastic fan, offering me observations that ultimately found their way into my final drafts.

My older sister Yolande was not surprised when I told her that our mother read my novels. "Mummy used to be a voracious reader," she said. She told me that Mummy would have her running back and forth to the library to get books for her. Within days after she borrowed one book for her, my mother would want another. "Eventually, I'd bring her stacks of books," Yolande told me.

How had I missed this? How had I never seen my mother reading a book? What had happened? Had I simply taken for granted that men were intellectually superior to women and so it would not be surprising that my mother's interests did not extend beyond the domestic affairs of her home and the activities of her circle of friends? And yet I had ambitions for myself. I wanted to be more than a mother and a wife; I wanted to be a writer. I had read Virginia Woolf. I wanted a room of my own and the means to be independent.

The women's movement had not yet reached our shores when I was young, before I left for college in America, but I had a grandmother who entertained artists and intellectuals in her home. She was good friends with Beryl McBurnie, who would later be awarded the Order of the British Empire (the OBE) for the playhouse she founded, the Little Carib Theater, which survives today as a showcase for local playwrights, actors, visual artists, dancers, and musicians.

I must have been ten years old when I first met Ms. McBurnie. She strode into my grandmother's drawing room wearing a shockingly bright multicolored cotton dress, shocking because I was accustomed to seeing women of Ms. McBurnie's social class in the more muted colors of the English dresses we imitated. But splashed across Ms. McBurnie's dress were the vivid colors of our tropical flora and fauna: reds, oranges, yellows, greens, purples, blues. Soon Ms. McBurnie began expostulating on the bold plans she had to form her own dance group and theater company. She was tired of all those English jigs and Scottish reels she had been taught at school, she declared. She wanted us to sing and play our own music and perform our own dances; she wanted to validate what she heard in the country from the people who were largely untouched by the British influence: the Africans, Caribs, French, Spaniards, Portuguese, many of them speaking a sort of patois, African words and rhythms laced with English. She talked about one of her concerts where her dancers performed a market scene shouting out the names of our local fruit: sapodilla, mango, pommerac, pomme cythère, chenet.

At nine years old my reading had been largely confined to the young adult novels by the English mystery writer Enid Blyton. I was consumed with the adventures of English boys and girls my age who picnicked on beaches without coconut trees, eating cucumber sandwiches and all sorts of exotic fruit—apples, peaches, pears, grapes—as they solved mysteries that eluded adult detectives. I used to do my best to emulate them, but try as I did, I never seemed able to develop a taste for cucumber sandwiches and always found the beaches where I had my picnics too hot to wear a cardigan. After I heard Ms. McBurnie, my imagination expanded. Cucumber sandwiches, apples, peaches, pears, and grapes didn't seem so special anymore, and I found myself being given permission to dream up picnics at the beach with pelau, coconut water, tamarind balls, pomme cythère, and mangoes.

I knew about other women, my aunts' contemporaries, who were challenging the roles traditionally assigned to females. Audrey Layne Jeffers, another of my grandmother's friends, founded the Coterie of Social Workers, and together with other women, established homes for the elderly, for the blind, for "women in distress," and nurseries for babies. Leonora Pujadas McShine—Leo, as she was familiarly known—organized the first League of Women Voters in Trinidad. My aunt Pearl, while still in her thirties, founded the Negro Theatre Workshop in London and was an agent there for artists of color.

So my ignorance of my mother's interest in books cannot be blamed on prejudices I inherited about the inferiority of women. Perhaps I was so brainwashed by the myth of Nunez intellectual superiority that I chose to be blind to much of what my mother did and said.

My mother told me the story about the first time she felt belittled by my father. I was in my fifties when she told me this, old enough to know better, and yet I was alarmed that my father would have dared to give voice to suspicions I had harbored, when I was a child, about her limited intellectual capacities.

It was true, my mother said: she had not been a reader. In fact, before she was married, she had never read a book from cover to cover. Then, one day, as she was talking idly about some social event that had taken place, my father snapped at her: "For God's sake, Una, is that all you can talk about? Educate yourself! Broaden your interests. At least read the newspaper!"

The irony, though, was that the newspaper was the most my father ever read, with one exception. He got a kick out of the novels of P.G. Wodehouse. After a day at work having to endure the arrogance of his British colonial bosses, little gave him as much pleasure as laughing at the buffoonish Bertie Wooster. But he never progressed beyond Wodehouse, or the newspapers (the cartoons were his favorite). My mother, on the other hand, took his admonishment to heart. When I discovered she had read my first novel, I gave her not only my other novels, but also novels by my favorite authors, novels that before my father began to withdraw from the world I could not imagine she was capable of appreciating or understanding. Within weeks she devoured Jane Austen's *Pride and Prejudice*, Gabriel García Márquez's *Love in the Time of Cholera*, V.S. Naipaul's *A House for Mr. Biswas*. (I would not count Naipaul among my favorite authors but *A House for Mr. Biswas* is as close to a masterpiece as a novel can get.) She read Naipaul's *A Way in the World* too, a novel I found difficult to digest, but she was intrigued by it and had lots of questions for me.

I dared to introduce her to my love of opera. I took her to see *Master Class* on Broadway, that backhanded homage to Maria Callas. Callas is at the end of her operatic career. She has lost her voice, her lover has abandoned her, and now she teaches opera hopefuls at Juilliard. She is angry, her voice shrill and strident, her young students cowering under her criticism of their slightest mistakes, and yet in the background we hear that miraculous voice that awed the world and made millions worship her.

My mother sat forward in her seat, her eyes glued to the stage. Was it the savagery of time marching indiscriminately onward, reducing us to shadows of our former selves, that had moved her, or regret for the person she could have been had her life not been circumscribed by eleven needy children and fourteen pregnancies? She wanted me to play arias by Callas when we got home, and as Callas's voice swelled throughout my house— "Casta Diva," "La Mamma Morta," my favorites—my mother and I bonded in a way we never had when I was young and living in her home. She returned to New York for the Christmas holidays, and I had no trouble persuading her to come along with me to Carnegie Hall to hear Handel's *Messiah*, though I warned her it was hours long. She sat transfixed through the entire program while my father, who comes from a musical family and played the violin as a boy, paced the corridors long after the first intermission had ended.

I want to think my father recognized this change in his wife and that their conversations had deepened beyond the mundane as they grew older together. If this was true, my mother, too, must have missed our father's searing intelligence that had made our world less chaotic, more ordered, safe. How frightened she must have been when he swirled butter in his tea, or when he insisted on going alone for the long walks he loved to take through the maze of streets in their neighborhood, wielding a stick to keep the stray dogs at bay. He always returned, but it must have been harrowing for my mother, waiting, as the minutes ticked away. She reacted in the only way she could. She buried her fear so deep that she was able pretend it did not exist. She chastised my father when he returned; she blamed him for making her miserable; she called him a selfish old man who cared only for himself.

If only she could see him now when I tell him that the funeral director has agreed to allow us come to the funeral parlor later in the morning. He is sitting up on the bed, eyes alert, the old intelligence shining out of them. In a voice crisp, clear, strong, he thanks me. "I can't wait to see her," he says.

If my mother were here now she would know that she was right: she had not lost him. Behind that jumble of memories in his brain, he has kept a clear space for her. He has never forgotten that he loves her.

II

Jacqueline returns just as my father and I are about to leave the house. I had picked out my father's clothes for him; I didn't want to take the chance he would put on the tuxedo again. He is dressed appropriately in a charcoal-gray suit, blue shirt, navy- and light-blue striped tie, black socks, black shoes. He looks handsome, as handsome as the day he and my mother renewed their marriage vows on their sixtieth wedding anniversary and shocked us all when they kissed each other on the mouth, something we had never before seen them do.

Jacqueline offers to bring us to the funeral parlor. I am still nervous about driving on the Trinidad roads and so I am happy to relinquish the car keys to her. She will go inside with us, she says, dismissing my warning that the funeral director explicitly requested that only my father and I come.

As a former banker and a novitiate at a convent, Jacqueline is a curious amalgam of both the technocrat who interprets the world through the cold logic of numbers, and the rabid spiritualist whose convictions are based largely on faith. It is the technocrat who guides us through the doors of the funeral parlor. I see my mother lying stiff and silent in the rose-pink dress I bought her, thinking back, as I took it off the rack at Bloomingdale's, how much she would love it, imagining her wearing it to a meeting of her ladies club, showing off both the dress and her daughter's fine taste. My knees turn to jelly. I turn away. I cannot approach the coffin. I lean against the wall in the back of the room, unable to speak, unable to be the support I wanted to be for my father.

Jacqueline takes charge. She puts her hand under my father's elbow and walks with him to the front of the room to view his wife. *View* is the word that enters my mind, for the object raised on the dais is not my mother but a representation of her.

My father stands next to the coffin. He looks down, nods, looks up again, and says in a loud, clear voice, "Well, that's that."

That's that? I am shaken out of the grief that left me speechless. "Oh, Daddy," I say, and step toward him, but he has already turned away from the coffin.

"I'm ready to go," he declares.

For a split second, I think he must mean he is ready to die. "No, Daddy," I say, and reach for his hand. But I am wrong. That is not at all what he means.

Jacqueline, who has not misinterpreted him for an instant, nods her head. "Yes, we should go now. Petra has made lunch for you. It's probably getting cold."

That's that. My father has the indisputable evidence he wanted. Now he is ready for lunch.

12

My mother belonged to a ladies club. She confessed to me one day that she was the youngest person in the group. If the women knew her age, they would put her out, she said. I disagreed. They like her for who she is, not for how old she is, I argued. "Oh, that's because they think I'm their age," she replied. "But if they knew . . . I mean, there are one or two ladies in the club who could be my daughters." I asked her why it mattered that she was the eldest among them. "It's about the way people think," she explained. "People think an older person will be old-fashioned, too fixed in her ways. Won't be able to understand their problems. My body may be old, but I don't feel any different from how I felt when I was young. I'm interested in new things the same way I was interested in new things when I was young. This body of ours betrays us. Inside, I'm the Una I always was. People judge you by your outsides, Elizabeth."

Guilty as charged, though she had not charged me, though she had not known of that incident with my grandmother when my grandmother's age was all the evidence I needed to judge her, to determine what she could do and could not do. How she should live.

I was twenty-two, recently returned to my island home with my newly minted bachelor's degree from

college in America, a Miss Know-It-All brimming with
the confidence, the hubris of youth. My grandfather
had died just weeks before, and I had come to visit my
grandmother, to commiserate with her, to console her.
*How will she manage now that her partner in life for more than
seventy years is not here to help her?* There was a scattering
of people across her front yard, all men—workmen, I
could see as I came closer, in work clothes, rumpled
shirts, stained and frayed work pants. Had they come
to clear out my grandparents' house, sent by scaven-
gers imagining my grandmother helpless, left to the
mercy of charities?

Hearing one of the men announce my arrival, my
grandmother popped her head out of the second-floor
window. "Oh, it's you, Elizabeth," she called out gaily.
"Come, come up!" And before I could answer, the cushions from her morris chairs came sailing to the ground,
barely missing me. I could hear her chastising the workmen who had thrown them down. "Idiots! You almost
hit my granddaughter on her head."

I joined in. "Wait!" I yelled at them. "Stop! I'm coming up. Granny, don't let them do this."

It took my grandmother seconds to understand we
were speaking at cross-purposes. She *wanted* the men to
throw out the cushions; they were old, smelly, she explained to me. She was having new ones made; she was
refurbishing her house.

"You think because I'm eighty-two I don't want to
live like you want to live? I have life in front of me, just
like you."

She was starting over. She was interested in new
things as I was interested in new things. I had judged

her by her outsides; I had done as my mother had feared the world would do.

But by her outsides, my mother fit perfectly in the company of the women in her club. Most of them dyed their hair to cover the gray. For years my mother dyed her hair too, but after the chemo made her bald, she was afraid of putting chemicals on her head. Yet even gray, snow-white in fact, she still looked younger than her ninety years. Her hips had spread, her arms were fleshy, the left arm perpetually swollen from the aftereffects of the surgery to remove her cancerous left breast. The varicose veins on her legs, the result of fourteen pregnancies, were blue and knotted, but her face was as smooth and as wrinkle-free as that of a woman thirty years her junior.

The mortician at the funeral parlor found it hard to believe she was ninety. "Not a wrinkle," she remarked. It was true. Except for the gutters that ran down the sides of her nose and her mouth, gutters I have inherited, there was little on my mother's face to mark her age.

"A woman who would tell her age would tell you everything," my mother once said. "Beware of that woman. She is a gossip; she cannot be trusted."

I am a writer. My business is to tell everything. My siblings are wary; they say I cannot be trusted with the family's secrets. They watch me carefully when I am in the company of others and the conversation turns to our family. I get a swift kick under the table, an elbow jabbed into my sides, if I embark on what they think should be a private family matter. *Keep skeletons in the closet. Don't wash your dirty linen in public.* Aphorisms they live by, but here I am, telling all, writing the all I think is all.

I do not share my sisters' obsession with privacy. *Obsession* is probably too strong a word; *conviction* would be more accurate. I do not share my sisters' conviction that it is foolhardy to expose oneself to the world. My sisters will allow the world to see only what they want people to see. This attitude, some say, is the legacy of slavery. They point to Paul Laurence Dunbar's poem "We Wear the Mask."

> *Why should the world be overwise,*
> *In counting all our tears and sighs?*
> *Nay, let them only see us, while*
> *We wear the mask.*

Perhaps there is some validity to this position, but the colonial experience suggests an alternative. In the colonies we were taught to love and admire the Mother Country. Even Caliban grudgingly admits to Prospero: *Thou . . . madest much of me / . . . and then I loved thee.* So perhaps this compulsion to dissimulate is the legacy of Victorian mores we willingly and enthusiastically mimicked— though the colonial officials we imitated were themselves mimics, sycophantic aspirants to the class of their superiors in England.

My sisters speak to me, however, of discretion. It is, they say, citing Shakespeare, the better part of valor. Yet I think it takes no little courage to open oneself to the world, to suffer the slings and arrows, so to speak, in the quest of knowing and being one's true self.

The professions I have chosen, or have chosen me, suit me perfectly. I am a professor; I am a fiction writer. Both require me to speak the truth, to make clear what

I think, what I believe, what I know. I think omission is as dishonest as commission. The thing deliberately unsaid is as much a distortion of the truth as a falsehood deliberately uttered.

Some of my colleagues in academia say that my role as a professor is to help students discover what they, the students, think. They object to a classroom arrangement where the professor stands at a lectern or sits at a desk, with students in a row in front of her. They find the circle more democratic, more conducive to learning. Put students in a circle, some of my colleagues say, and they begin to talk to each other; they begin to learn that their views are not the only ones; they begin to see alternatives.

I do not disagree, but I think there is merit in the etymology of my title. I am a professor. *Profiteri*: to lay claim to, to declare openly. I am supposed to profess something, and the something I am supposed to profess is a result of years of study and analysis. I have tried the circle; it works sometimes, but not always. Of the various insights attributed to Steve Jobs, the one I most connect to is his position regarding focus groups. Walter Isaacson ends his biography of the man in Jobs's own words:

> *Some people say, "Give the customers what they want." But that's not my approach. Our job is to figure out what they're going to want before they do. I think Henry Ford once said, "If I'd asked customers what they wanted, they would have told me, 'A faster horse!'" People don't know what they want until you show it to them. That's why I never rely on market research. Our task is to read things that are not yet on the page.*

I'm not so unbending. I believe that my role as an educator is to lead out as well as to lead in: *ex*, the Latin for out; *ducere*, meaning to lead. I want to bring out the talents my students are capable of realizing, but I do so by teaching them what I know and why I have come to the conclusions I profess. I talk, I reveal, I empty myself; I share with them my knowledge, my convictions, my doubts. I want them to take the baton I pass on to them—my years of study and reflection—and run with it into the future. I want them to surpass me, to add their own thoughts, their own analyses to mine, and arrive at conclusions I have not yet conceived. I want them to challenge me. I admit I am impatient with some educators who seem to put methods before subject matter. In a recent respectable journal focused on pedagogy, a professor advised teachers to take a class in theater, as he had done. His acting skills improved his teaching performance, the professor gushed. But I have seen too many teachers use the classroom as a theater where their students are a captive audience and the instructors get to perform on stage, telling jokes, relating stories from their experiences, commenting on current news or popular TV shows their students watch. These teachers claim they are simply using a method to engage bored students, but too often the bell rings for the end of class and little content has filtered through.

Perhaps learning a craft can improve one's skills, but I don't believe it can make you an artist, no more than I believe that imparting theories and practices can make you a master teacher. I don't promise my students in my creative writing workshops that I can turn them into talented writers. I promise to teach them the craft; I promise to teach them all I know; I promise to show them styles and techniques of our most successful writers. I tell them the talent will come from them, from their unique way of seeing the world. I share the view of Martin, a colleague of the fictive writer and teacher John Coetzee (is he really fictive?) in J.M. Coetzee's autobiographical novel *Summertime*. In response to a question about John Coetzee's aptitude for teaching, Martin comments: "I would say that one teaches best what one knows best and feels most strongly about." He goes on to be critical of John Coetzee, who, he says, "knew a fair amount about a range of things, but not a great deal about anything in particular," and whose "depth of his involvement [in his subjects] did not come out in his teaching." This, I take it, is J.M. Coetzee's reflection on his effectiveness as a teacher, and the importance he places on both knowledge and passion.

I think teacher education programs will be best served by grounding prospective teachers in the subjects they intend to teach. I think a thorough knowledge of their subjects will serve them a million times better than all the strategies of delivery. I think teachers are effective when they view themselves as students of their subjects, motivated by a continuous desire to learn more. The passion a teacher has for her subject shines through and students get infected by her enthusiasm in much the same way as one catches a cold when one's neighbor sneezes and you have the misfortune of droplets of the virus spraying on you. I fell in love with T.S. Eliot because I got infected by my literature professor's passion for his poetry. She sat at her desk the entire semester, never standing, never moving from her place even once. The notion of forming a circle with us would never have entered her head, nor would the idea of engaging us with juicy stories about contemporary events. She was a nun, more or less cloistered in her convent. She rarely watched TV, and never read the tabloids. Yet she infected me so thoroughly I continue to read Eliot to this day.

It is my passion to discover who I am, and why I am here in this world, that drives me to write fiction. And I am convinced that discovering the who and the why can happen only if I tell all.

One of my most influential mentors was the African American writer John Oliver Killens. I didn't always agree with his theories about fiction writing, but this one stuck with me. He said to me: "You will not be a writer, Elizabeth, until you are willing to take off your clothes at high noon in the middle of the town square." That admonition hovered over me as I tried to write my first novel.

I was in my late thirties at the time, one of the many beneficiaries of the hard-won victories of the women's movement. Much had changed for women but so rapidly that I found myself buffeted by waves that pushed me out to the wide-open sea before dashing me back onshore, my skin scraping against the coarse sand. I wanted to be a free and independent woman, earning my own livelihood, charting my own life, and yet my sense of self, my identity as a woman, was inextricably tied to my ability to fulfill the roles of wife, mother, and homemaker that had defined success for my mother and for so many women before her.

The women of my generation were in unchartered

waters. We were pioneers, crossing seas and landscapes our mothers had never traveled. I had gone to university and then on to graduate school. I had earned a PhD in English at New York University's School of Arts and Science, at that time a rarity for women, especially black women. In fact, I was one of only two women of color in my graduating class, the other an immigrant like me, but from a privileged caste in India. My mother, on the other hand, had barely finished secondary school. Then, too, I was working full time as an assistant professor at Medgar Evers College, a unit of the City University of New York.

With the exception of one year, my mother had not worked outside of the home. It was not her choice: she was terminated—fired—when she got pregnant with her second child. She would have been fired when she got pregnant with me, her first biological child, but her boss liked her and found a loophole to keep her as his assistant. When the swelling in her stomach began to show the second time, his hands were tied. There was a rule in the colonial government that married women should not be permitted to work, particularly married women with children. On the face of it, the ruling appeared to be protective of women: men, the logic went, should assume responsibility for taking care of their wives and children. But in fact the prohibition against married women in the workforce ensured that men would continue to hold the reins of power.

Raising eleven children probably would have made working outside the home difficult, if not impossible, for my mother. Still, she did not have to raise us by herself. There were neighbors in our town who looked out for us, who had permission to reprimand us, to set us straight in her absence. There were relatives who lived nearby, next door or a bicycle ride, a bus ride away. I had no such assistance raising two boys, my son and my ex-husband's five-year-old son. I was an immigrant living in a strange land among strange people. With the exception of my friend Mary Taylor, it would be years before I would find American friends I could count on to help me from the kindness of their hearts.

So there were fundamental differences between my mother's life and mine. I resented the obstacles in my way as I tried to climb the ladder in a university system still dominated by men, and yet I was hounded by my failure to measure up to the standards my mother had set as a homemaker, wife, and mother. When I first found the courage to dare to conceive I could write a novel, my immediate thought was that I would write about a woman facing my dilemma, a woman trying to straddle the demands of work and home. But each time I began to write this novel, I found myself stalled. I couldn't write about this woman, not because I had not experienced her life, but because I didn't know the woman who was narrating the story; I didn't know who I was.

I had been taught in school to love all things British. Everything I knew about the geography of my island had been taught to me by my father and grandfather, both hunters and lovers of nature. But I had studied the geography of the British Empire, the other places the British had colonized, lessons intended to reinforce the myths of British superiority. "The sun never sets" on British soil, Churchill had boasted. Then, too, I knew next to nothing about writers from the Caribbean region. V.S. Naipaul was just being published when I was entering high school and his early works did little to counter the prevailing view the colonizer had of us: we were a buffoonish people, mimic men, the butt of jokes, the stuff of farce and satire.

Incredibly, I was nineteen, in college, in the US, before I truly understood the extent to which slavery had existed on my island. Those were the heady days of the civil rights movement. African Americans were digging into their past and they retrieved mine. I was horrified to learn about the cruelty of the British, for what I knew about our island's history was what they had taught me: they had come to our island and blessed us with their culture and largesse. Like Caliban, we were expected to be grateful.

I remember cringing when my high school teacher in Trinidad, a white European, read to the class those lines by Prospero chastising Caliban for his ingratitude:

> I pitied thee,
> Took pains to make thee speak, taught thee each hour
> One thing or other: when thou didst not, savage,
> Know thine own meaning, but wouldst gabble like
> A thing most brutish, I endowed thy purposes
> With words that made them known.

Could it be true? Was it possible that before the British came, my people were savages who had no discernible language of their own, no words to make their meaning known? Should I be grateful to the British for teaching me? I was a student in a school the British had

Meester Zebra

68703 Perez Rd, STE A1
Cathedral City, CA
92234-7221
(760) 459-3325
meesterzebra.com

Sep 7, 2022
2:15 PM

Albino

Ticket: #13

Authorization: 224253

Receipt: xODi

Mastercard Debit

AID A0 00 00 04 10 10 10

TO GO

Cubano Sandwich x 1

Fries

Subtotal	$13.99
Sales Tax	$1.22

Total	$15.21
MasterCard 4111 (Chip)	$15.21

Suzanne M Seymour

founded; they had sent their teachers to educate me. But I had not yet read George Lamming's *The Pleasures of Exile*. I had yet to fully understand the influence of perspective, of point of view. Years later I would tell Caliban's side of the story. In my novel *Prospero's Daughter*, which I purposely set the year before our independence from England, Carlos allows me to say how I felt to be torn between gratitude and resentment, at one moment admiring the achievements of the British people and full of appreciation for their contributions to my island— the systems of government, education, and law they established—and at the next burning with anger for the power they wielded over our lives, leaving us unsure of our identity, doubting the value of our culture, the relevance of our history.

Still, I fell in love with British literature, my attachment having roots similar to the Roman adulation of the cultural achievements of the Greeks. The Romans had conquered Greece with their mighty physical prowess, but ironically it was the Greeks with their philosophical tracts, scientific experiments, artistic achievements, and great works of literature who were the real colonizers, shaping the ideas and creative arts of the ancient Roman world.[1]

I was raised with the literature of the English colonizers. I was familiar of course with our folktales, but my exposure was limited to the times when my family went to the countryside on holiday and I had occasion to hear our storytellers recount them. We lived on the outskirts of our capital, the hub of the colonial govern-

---

1. See Stephen Greenblatt's magnificent book *The Swerve: How the World Became Modern* (New York: W.W. Norton & Company, 2011) for more about this ironic twist on how the conquered became the true colonizer.

ment ministries, not far from where the Nobel laureate V.S. Naipaul lived. I went to the girls equivalent of his boys school in the city. We both had a British education in the tradition of the best British public schools.

Today, the English poet John Keats consoles me when a melancholy fit falls upon me and I am buffeted by the illogic of the transience of this life. Wordsworth reminds me of the beauties of nature; I laugh with Chaucer as he pokes fun at the follies of the church. Shakespeare never ceases to teach me about our human condition, our triumphs and our flaws. I revel in the music of his poetry, the magic of his imagery. Because of Jane Austen, I can count on one hand the people who still call me by my childhood name Betty. I was eleven when I first read *Pride and Prejudice.* Until then, my family and friends addressed me as Betty, the diminutive of my real name. But I had identified with Elizabeth Bennet. She was no diminutive, neither a diminutive Bennet nor a diminutive woman. She stood up to her father who was easily able to belittle her mother and sisters with his witty, sarcastic tongue. I admired Elizabeth's spunk and independence and wanted to be just like her, so I forbade my parents and siblings from calling me Betty. I was to be Elizabeth from then on.

In my arsenal of the writer's craft and the art of storytelling, I fiercely protect what I have learned from these British writers. They continue to be my most influential teachers. I am grateful, too, to the British for making me memorize long passages from their literature, which to this day I can recall in an instant and are a comfort to me. Yes, I am grateful to the British colonizers for this, for this literature, but not because it is the literature of their people, but because it is the literature of the human race to which I belong. Because it is part of the human heritage and so mine.

But for years, when I was a child, I rooted for Tarzan, willingly suspending not only disbelief but all logical thinking. For even a child knows it does not make sense that a European man, unaccustomed to the heat and humidity of the African rainforest, practically naked, wearing only a skimpy loincloth and carrying no weapons of any kind, would be able to kill the most ferocious animals with his bare hands (a hungry lion, for God's sake!) and outwit natives with their poisonous arrows. And yet I never doubted Tarzan's prowess, never doubted his right (God-given?) to rule the jungle.

In the creative writing workshop I took with John O. Killens, he would make his point to us, aspiring writers, about the value of fiction, especially fiction by writers of color, by referring to the universal image children seemed to have of Tarzan. "Tarzan will continue to be the king of the jungle," he would say, "until the lion learns how to speak."

My paternal grandmother—God bless her soul—was a fierce Anglophile. How could she not be? Her father was an Englishman, though we know with a name like Fitt, he was most likely one of those Irishmen from Northern Ireland who swore fidelity to the English Crown. He had a proper English wife, of course, and proper English children, but he had sired several more children with the local women, including my grandmother's mother. It seemed he loved her best. He gave her children his name and kept her in style. My sister Judith has a photograph of my grandmother when she was about twelve or so. Her skin is white, her hair is blond, two long plaits that fall over her shoulders. She is standing next to her mother, an elegant woman with polished black skin who is dressed in Victorian finery. My grandmother, too, is wearing a beautiful lace dress that clutches her neck and falls down to her ankles. Her dress is white; her dark-skinned mother's dress is black. Was this choice of color deliberate? I can only guess at an answer.

An Anglophile, my grandmother had nothing but scorn for the Catholic Church and loathing for the practitioners of obeah and voodoo. The Catholic Church was ruled by Rome, not England, and the practitioners of obeah and voodoo insisted on holding on to their links to Africa, to our "savage past." In her defense I would say that my grandmother's loyalty to England stopped with her children. When it became obvious to her that her darker-skinned children—my father in particular—was discriminated against both in school and at work, she did not hold back her tongue.

So what were my beliefs? Who was I? The color of my skin linked me to Africa, but my beliefs and attitudes seemed grounded in the beliefs and attitudes of the people who had colonized my island. I could not begin to write a novel until I had untangled these threads that left me uncertain of my identity. The first novel I wrote had to lead me on the path to self-discovery.

It happened that I was awarded a fellowship from the National Endowment for the Humanities to study at Yale with the late Michael Cooke, who was conducting a seminar entitled "African Patterns of Thought." That seminar would be a pivotal point in my development as a person and a writer. It confirmed for me the accuracy of George Lamming's contentions in *The Pleasures of Exile*. There are ways of seeing, of viewing the world, of arriving at the truth through routes other than the ones I had been taught by my teachers and my church. I began to write a novel set in late-nineteenth-century Trinidad, before oil was discovered in the south of the island. I wanted to know why families such as mine who owned cocoa lands in the south had not become rich. I had discovered they'd either sold the land or abandoned it. I wanted to know why. What logic or pattern of thinking had they used to make their decision?

I remembered the stories my father had told me about his hunting days, how he found his way out of the forest in the thick of night. He would make a flambeau by wrapping a piece of cloth around a stick, dipping it in one of the pools of oil that he could find almost anywhere among the cocoa trees, putting a match to it, and lighting his way to safety. "Didn't your family own some of this land?" I asked him. I knew his Portuguese grandfather worked on a cocoa plantation, and after he died, his wife—my father's grandmother—inherited some of the land. "Yes," my father said, and before I could ask the obvious question, he added, "but who knew about the value of oil in those days? The British were heating their homes with coal from Newcastle and Ford had not yet built his motorcars. World War I had not yet happened. Who knew they'd need oil to fuel the bombers?"

Who knew? No one had a crystal ball. So what would you do if the cocoa trees on your land were being destroyed by the oil that was surfacing around their roots? Cocoa was a main source of income for the planters, but now they were facing the end of their livelihood.

What if you were a planter and someone offered to buy your land, someone who had no notion of the insidious oily substance silently choking the life out of your trees? Would you sell the land? Logic, scientific thinking, would lead you to do just that. How clever you would be to sell the land before the trees died! How foolish the buyer would have been not to have done his research! But what if you decided to consult the resident obeah-man before making your decision? This was the question I chose to pursue in my first novel, *When Rocks Dance*.

I had read *Oedipus Rex*. Oedipus goes to the prophet Tiresias for advice on the cause of the plague that is devastating his people. And Tiresias lashes out at him: "You are the curse, the corruption of the land!" In my novel the local landowner consults the obeahman whose response is just as scathing. It is you, you are the cause of the plague infecting your cocoa lands, the obeahman says to the landowner. The oil destroying your cocoa lands is a sign from the gods, a message that you have offended them in some way. To save his cocoa plantation, the landowner needs to examine his soul, he needs to find out what he had done wrong in his life and make amends, make a sacrifice to the gods. But above all, the obeahman warns the landowner, do not sell your land, for the earth does not belong to man; the earth belongs to the gods. This, of course, is not logical, scientific thinking; it's magical, mystical thinking, but it leads to the truth about the importance of self-examination, of cleansing one's soul, of making reparations. It is telling too of the respect we should have for our planet. And there is material reward for this way of thinking, for this way of seeing the world. Because if the landowner holds on to his land, he and the generations to follow will have riches far more than they could ever have imagined.

When I came home, to Trinidad, for the celebration of the publication of *When Rocks Dance*, my sister Jacqueline pulled me aside. Her face feverish, her eyes darting with fear, she whispered hoarsely in my ear, "All that obeah business you wrote about, Elizabeth, you don't believe it, do you?"

I did my best to calm her down. "It's a novel," I responded. "Fiction. Make-believe."

But I could tell she was not convinced. In the Caribbean the fit was perfect between African and Amerindian spiritual retentions and Catholic mysticism. Statues, lighted candles, indulgences, prayers for the dead, the transubstantiation of bread and wine into the body and blood of Christ that was eaten and drunk at Mass had their appeal to memories hardwired in the genetic coding of people who had used sacrifice, symbols, and prayer to appease their gods. My sister was afraid there could be some truth in the story I told.

And there was. I would not go to an obeahman, I said, putting her at ease, but in writing this novel I discovered that there are other routes to the truth. I found a new respect for my African past, for the beliefs of my ancestors denigrated by the British colonial masters. I came closer than I had ever been to knowing who I am, to knowing myself.

I remain a seeker of truth, a position that has not always served me well. I say too much, my sisters claim. Today, though, I find myself useful to them. In the fog of grief, my sisters divvy up responsibilities according to our professions. The ones with business acumen will discuss finances with the funeral director; the ones with medical backgrounds will gather details from the hospital about my mother's last hours; the more religious of us will speak to the parish priest to arrange a suitable Mass—nothing less than a High Mass, to be sure. The ones who understand Caribbean protocol and style— that is, the ones who have remained in the Caribbean—will be in charge of the flowers, the program at the church and at the cemetery, the meal that will follow the internment, the guests to be invited to our parents' home.

I am the writer in the family. My siblings choose me to draft my mother's eulogy. They are not in the state of mind to weigh the risks of putting this assignment in the hands of someone who exposes too much. They do not give me specific instructions, but I know what they want. They want hagiography, something flowery, something that leaves no doubt about the goodness of our mother. Something that will not embarrass them. "Elizabeth knows grammar," they say. "She teaches composition. Let her do it." They leave the wording in my "capable hands."

13

My sister-in-law Beverly finds Mary; I finally remembered the name of the cruise ship. With just this little information and using all her contacts, my sister-in-law has managed to persuade the cruise line to let my sister off the ship so that she can come to Trinidad.

Mary arrives in a flood of tears. The moment she spots me, she runs toward me and throws her arms around my neck, practically strangling me. Tears flow steadily down her cheeks and onto my back, dampening my blouse. Her sobs are loud, rasping. I stand against her, stiff with shock. Unaccustomed to such displays of emotion, my body freezes.

The Nunezes carry on; they pick up the pieces; they move forward. "Well, that's that," my father said when he viewed his wife's body. It was over; the past belongs to the past. No use crying over spilled milk. But Mary collapses against me, her chest pressed into mine, her tears coming so rapidly and with such volume she chokes on her breath. Words on the tip of her tongue come out as unintelligible gibberish. All I can distinguish are snorts, gasps, gurglings.

My father used to tell us a joke about an English overseer and an inexperienced worker to bring home his point about the futility of lamenting something you have no power to change. An English overseer was out carousing with friends, leaving the local brown-skinned worker with the job of boiling the sugarcane juices until sugar crystals began to form. This was not a job for an inexperienced man such as this one. Soon the poor man found himself with a hard brown clotted mess on hands. When the Englishman came back, he greeted his worker. "So how was your day, old man?" "Well, massa," the man replied, "what ent bile (boil) yet, ent spile (spoil) yet; what biling, spiling; and what done bile, done spile."

My father repeated that joke to us dozens of times. What has already boiled has already spoiled. The results are irreversible. Nothing can be done to turn that brown clotted mess into sugar crystals. This is a lesson my father very much wanted us to learn. We can do nothing to bring our mother back to life. *That's that.*

The Nunezes do not break down; they do not let misfortune stand in their way. When I came simpering to my father about my poor grades, complaining that I had studied hard, expecting him to sympathize, he responded with Mark Antony's eulogy to Caesar: "Ambition should be made of sterner stuff."

My great-great-grandfather had soldiered on though he was enslaved, but once freed, he made sure my great-grandmother, Ann Rose Dormor, his only daughter, was educated even if that meant driving her to school by horse and buggy through muddy country roads four hours a day. Ann Rose soldiered on when her husband died and she lost her only means of financial support. She baked pies and cakes and sold them at the market in St. Joseph. She had to take my grandfather out of school because she could not afford the fees, and because she needed his help to take the baked goods to the market in St. Joseph, a distance of six miles from her home that my grandfather had to travel by foot. Luckily, a Chinese shopkeeper there was so impressed by my grandfather's intelligence that he offered to pay for his education; my grandfather was able to finish school at the top of his class.

My grandparents, Antonio and Georgiana Nunez, soldiered on too, though the colonial bosses did their best to throw obstacles in their way. Education was the only escape from a future of menial labor in colonial Trinidad, and my grandparents, like my great-grandparents and my great-great-grandfather newly freed from slavery, were determined their children would not be at the beck and call of some ignorant overseer. Their children would be educated; they would go to the best secondary schools on the island. The best ones were private schools and they were expensive. There were four: two for males and two for females. The oldest, established in the late 1800s for the children of the English colonizers and the French Creole plantation owners, were St. Mary's College for boys and St. Joseph's Convent for girls. Those were the schools where my grandparents intended to send their children.

They had nine—five sons and four daughters. When my grandfather was headmaster of the only school in the country district of Arouca, they had been able to pay the tuition for their two oldest sons, but when my father's turn came (he was their third child) my grandfather was sixty and at the age when all government civil servants were required to retire. My grandmother, who was much younger than my grandfather, pitched in. She bought a cow and hired a woman to milk it. She would sell the milk to pay for my father's tuition, she decided. So at four thirty every morning, in the deep darkness before dawn, my father had to wake up and get out of his bed to find the cow, which had been allowed to graze on any grassy field in the neighborhood, and tie it to a tree for the woman who would come to milk it. By five thirty, he had to be out of the house again to catch the bus for the hour-long ride to school in the city.

But there were other children to educate, so my grandfather returned to work as district warden of Diego Martin, and, later, as district water warden. He was sixty-five when he was forced to stop working again. By then my grandmother was bringing in more income, as postmistress of the district and, quite extraordinary for a woman of her time, as an entrepreneur. She could not drive, but she ran a taxi service. She rented one car and hired a driver, and soon she was renting more cars and collecting more fares. With my grandfather's paltry pension, and my grandmother's income, they were able to give the rest of their sons as well as their daughters the best education available on the island.

So my father knew a lot about sterner stuff. When his income was barely enough to feed us, he bought food on credit at the local grocery, something he so totally detested that he would never buy anything on credit again when his fortunes changed—but he did it in those early years to pay for private lessons for his children so they could compete for scholarships to the best private schools on the island. He was gentler on me and his other daughters than on his sons when we did not meet his expectations. I had to take the exhibition test twice—

the scholarship exam for high school—before I was successful. My father was sympathetic when I didn't succeed the first time. My brothers were successful on their first try; David was only ten, perhaps the youngest in his class, and yet I don't remember my father celebrating. "Study harder," he admonished his sons when they slipped from first or second place in class. "Ambition should be made of sterner stuff."

Where is Mary's sterner stuff now? She tightens her hold around my neck and I am left with no choice but to do the decent thing. I raise my arms from my sides and wrap them loosely around her body. Her tears continue to fall.

14

There were consequences. We have paid a price for this sterner stuff handed down from our great-great-grandparents to our great-grandparents, and then to our grandparents and our parents, and ultimately to us. I recount the wreckage of our marriages: nine ending in divorce or unresolved separations.

But surely we have been successful. We are doctors, business executives, actuaries; one of us is a lawyer, another an entrepreneur, another a midwife. I am a professor and a writer. Surely it has served us well to be made of sterner stuff. Surely our grandparents would have been proud of us. Not one of us has had to earn his or her living by menial labor, not one of us is at the beck and call of an English overseer.

My father was not ignorant of Mark Antony's intent. He understood the man meant to undermine Brutus. Brutus says he slew Caesar because Caesar was ambitious, and Mark Antony, master of irony, uses Brutus's very words to trap him. How was Caesar ambitious? Mark Antony asks the fickle crowd gathered for Caesar's funeral. Caesar shared his coffers with the people of Rome. He wept for the poor. *Ambition should be made of sterner stuff.*

Still, for my father there was wisdom in Mark Antony's words in spite of the malice lurking beneath them.

Surrendering to emotions might distract us from our goals, he warned us. We should be made of sterner stuff. And now there is Mary letting her guard down, weeping as if her world has come to an end.

This is not the first time I have seen Mary allow herself to be swept away by the feelings she has for our mother. I have seen her throw her arms around my mother's neck, and, once, in a burst of happiness, she flung herself into our mother's lap.

Mary had just got married and she and her husband, already mature adults, had agreed to remain in the countries where they felt most comfortable. For Mary's husband that meant Trinidad, in the countryside; for Mary, America, in the suburbs of New York's cities. On this occasion Mary had just returned to Trinidad to visit her husband. I also happened to be in Trinidad. We were gathered, my siblings and I, in our parents' bedroom as usual. Mary barged in, her face glowing, eyes shining, a wide smile on her lips, all learned restraint abandoning her in the whirlwind of happiness that had enveloped her from being with her husband again. Our mother was sitting in her armchair. Mary ran to her and plopped herself into her lap. Our mother froze. Her eyes shot open, her back stiffened. I could tell she was scared to death. She did not know what to say, what to do. Mary was like a baby in her arms, curled into the fetal position, wanting to be hugged, to be kissed. My heart bled for my mother. I laughed, a false laugh to be sure, but it broke the grip of terror that had turned my mother into a statue, her arms stiff at her sides, her mouth hanging open.

That was the last time I saw Mary kiss or hug our

mother like that. Now, as her chin digs deeper into the back of my shoulder, tears pouring down her cheeks, her arms like manacles around me, I realize suddenly I have been wrong. *Mary is crying for herself.* She is crying for *her* loss, not for the loss of our mother. She is grieving for the spaces left in her heart all those years when she was a child, when she was a young woman, spaces that not even her husband would be able to fill.

The repression of displays of affection has left us stunted, desperate for emotional comfort but unable to ask for it or know how to give it. And once in a while, as had happened to Mary, and is happening with her now, a dam breaks open.

I once asked my mother if she knew why her children were seemingly unable to sustain long-term romantic relationships. She shook her head. It made her unhappy that we had not stayed with our spouses, she said. She wished she could do something to change that.

David asked too. We were celebrating our parents' fiftieth wedding anniversary. When David's turn came to thank them for the life they had given us, he asked questions instead. "How were you able to stay married for so long? What is the secret to your long marriage?"

My father looked away, avoiding David's eyes. My mother simply smiled. David, his voice filled with sadness and wonder, addressed my mother directly: "They don't make women like you anymore."

David's second marriage was on life support; his wife had accused him of cheating on her.

My father had also cheated on my mother. Several times. She did not leave him.

Was my father's excuse the old canard that men

often offer? They wouldn't seek love elsewhere if they were shown love in the home.

Shall I blame the church? Shall I blame a church that forbade birth control, that for so many women stifled passion in the midst of lovemaking for fear of the consequences of more babies than they could manage? In this context, was my father's behavior understandable?

I think my siblings and I were needier, though. I think it must have been hard for our spouses to fill that yawning space left in our hearts from the attention we yearned for when we were children. Our need for love was not the ordinary need of mature adults; it was a kind of raw hunger for the unconditional love that babies demand. *Beloved's hunger.*

Were we asking for too much from our parents? There were limits to the time my father could be with us. He had to leave the house to earn the money to feed, clothe, and shelter us. And my mother? What more could she have done? She had her own needs too, her own hunger for attention from the man she loved. She would shut her bedroom door and lock it, but there were always little ones wailing outside, begging to be let in.

And she was ambitious. What and who could she have been if there hadn't been laws thwarting her ambitions, disapprobation cast upon her by a society that declared a woman's place to be in her home minding her husband and her children?

And was it possible to give love and attention to eleven children at the same time? How was my mother to share herself with a squealing baby who needed to be fed, a toddler burning up with fever, little children with cuts and bruises, pubescent boys and girls alarmed by their changing bodies, teenagers grappling with the surprise of raging hormones, sibling rivalries, mischiefs to be quelled, homework to supervise, etc., etc.? Only in *The Sound of Music* and other such movies are large families so well adjusted and happy. The Duggars on cable television tell a romantic version of the truth. Nineteen children and counting, but they have nannies and home assistants, and we are yet to learn how those children will fare once they have families of their own. Discovery Communications, the TLC Channel, and corporate sponsors furnished the Duggars's house, supplied them with all sorts of efficient gadgets, which, in ways my mother could not have imagined, reduced the drudgery of housework. The Duggars say they will have as many children as God will see fit to give them. If every couple had nineteen children and counting, there would not be sufficient resources on our planet Earth, created by this same God, to sustain us.

I continue to be amazed by the close relationship my son has with his two daughters, the attention and the tangible expressions of affection he gives to both of them. Just two daughters and yet my son, who is a thousand times less guarded than I am, whose capacity for empathy continues to astound me, is stretched thin by the effort it takes to reassure his two children of his love for them. How would he manage if he had eleven, if like my parents he had eleven hearts to fill?

My parents did what they thought was best. They prepared us to succeed in the world they knew, a world where your country was not your own and belonged to people who did not look like you, who lived far across the ocean in a distant, cold land. You had to be smart in such a world; you had to be alert; you had to be made of sterner stuff. The colonizer succeeds when he manages to colonize your mind. You cannot let your emotions derail you. You must guard your mind.

15

S till I continue to blame the church. I hold the church responsible too for constraining our emotional lives. The constant fear of pregnancy robbed my mother of much of the pleasure she could have had in sex, so it must have been difficult for her to find the space and calm in the center of her being to attend to our emotional needs when hers were wanting. Was it the threat of damnation that kept her tethered to her husband when he strayed?

"Women today aren't willing, like you were, to stay the course, to stick with the ups and downs in their marriage," David said to our mother.

But would she have been willing to stick with the downs in her marriage, her husband's infidelity, if she'd had the opportunities women have today, and her daughters have had, for advanced education and professional careers? I think she would have; I believe she would have stayed with her husband.

Yet my mother did not accept my father's infidelities passively. On more than one occasion I saw her get so angry with him that in the midst of a quarrel, her accusations getting louder and more strident, she snatched the tablecloth from the table while we were eating, sending plates, cups, saucers, cutlery, food flying across the room. Once when my father had not come home from one of his "meetings," though it was well past midnight, she waited for him behind the door with a pot in her hand. She was always remorseful afterward, ashamed of herself for her outbursts, but I think she must have felt trapped, hemmed in with no possibility of escape. I think she must have felt she had no other way of fighting back.

My father was always remorseful too. He never admitted any wrongdoing, but he also never retaliated. He let my mother rail at him, shatter plates on the floor, throw pots at him, call him names, and he kept his mouth shut. In the morning he was charming: "Una, why don't you make a pot of pelau, and we'll take the children to the beach?"

Why did my mother stay? The obvious answer is that she had no other means of supporting herself and her children. But she also loved her husband and I think because she loved him, she was willing to make this tacit agreement with him: so long as he did not embarrass her, she would do her best to look the other way. My father kept his side of the bargain. When he was in public with her, he was the soul of discretion, making it clear she was the only woman in his life. If there were whispers about his trysts, he denied them vehemently. This arrangement was by no means exceptional. Many marriages in my parents' day survived this way, and though I thought women were trapped by the restrictions imposed on them in the name of gentility and concern for their "fragile" sensibilities, it seemed to me that men were trapped too. I cannot say I felt sorry for them, but I did think there was pressure on men (in my part of the world anyway) to prove their virility by chalking up female conquests whether within or outside of marriage. Ultimately, though, it was the specter of burning in the red-hot flames of hell for all eternity that made my mother a willing partner in my father's deceptions. She could not, would not, leave him. She had sworn an oath before God to be a wife to her husband for better or worse. To break that oath was to commit a mortal sin which would plunge her into the fires of hell.

These were not the days of Newt Gingrich, when a man, married with children, commits adultery, remarries, commits adultery again, and then, because he wishes to marry his lover, who is Catholic and wants a grand Catholic wedding, manages to convince his priest, his bishop, and the gatekeepers at the Vatican that his two marriages, the first lasting eighteen years and producing two children, the second ending after nineteen years, were not marriages at all. He is in fact a free and single man, a bachelor, with every right to marry the woman he loves. No, in my mother's day, in the Caribbean island where she lived, the annulment of a marriage contract was unheard of. You married for life; you stayed with your spouse through thick and thin. In time an adulterous affair will run its natural course, the marriage will resume; children and grandchildren will be your reward.

It turned out that the two of my siblings who sought, and were granted, annulments of their marriages were the two who had seemed to me the most religious among us: a sister who was a novitiate in a convent, and a brother who had flirted with the possibility of becoming a priest. Each of their marriages had lasted for more than nineteen years; both of them had children; both had been able to convince the church that their marriage contracts were flawed, though my brother says it was his ex-wife, not he, who sought the annulment.

I had stayed in my marriage for my son, but in his last year in high school when he was getting ready to leave home for college and I should have been preparing finally to free myself from a marriage that had made me unhappy, I, who thought myself an independent thinker, a liberal, a feminist, who was repulsed by the hypocrisy of the church's stance on annulment which favored the rich and those with connections to the Catholic hierarchy, which kept the poor in bondage to unhappy and sometimes dangerous marriages, found myself aching for approbation from that very church, needing the blessing of my parish priest, his concurrence with me on the righteousness of my reasons for divorcing a husband of twenty years.

The divorced and remarried French ex-president Nicolas Sarkozy was reputed to have said that though he did not adhere to all the rules of the church, he was culturally Catholic. I, too, was then, and even now to a certain degree, culturally Catholic. How could I have been otherwise? I had been raised in a strict orthodox Catholic home and was taught by nuns in Catholic schools. I went to Mass every Sunday, confession every Saturday. During the forty days of Lent, I attended five o'clock Mass most mornings and made the stations of the cross on Fridays. Every night my siblings and I knelt down around our mother's bed to recite the rosary. Our Halloween was All Hallows' Eve. We didn't dress up in costumes; we went to the graves of our dead relatives and prayed for the release of their souls from purgatory.

We lit candles and put money in the slots next to the statues of saints and offered indulgences for the dearly departed. I remember praying for my Protestant paternal grandparents and my father's sisters and brothers who would surely be going to hell unless they converted to Catholicism. In fact, while I was still in secondary school, I had managed to convert an entire Chinese family.

Gitmee A— was my best friend in school. Her parents had immigrated to Trinidad from China and spoke barely intelligible English. I grieved for Gitmee and her family. It pained me to know that because my best friend was neither a Catholic nor a Christian, she would be sent to Limbo when she died, the place for the souls of the unbaptized. I wanted her to be in heaven with me. Somehow I convinced her, and she convinced her siblings, to convert. It was one of the happiest days of my childhood when I stood next to her and her family at the baptismal fount.

For years I wore a scapular around my neck, under my clothes, for the Blessed Virgin. I kept it on though the strings frayed and disintegrated and caused a perpetual rash of painful little bumps on my chest.

I joined the Legion of Mary. My duty was to comfort the poor and the dying. I was fourteen when I was sent to the Poor House, a stately colonial Victorian government building with arches and columns, outside a pristine lawn but inside scenes from a Dickens novel, the place reeking of filth and urine and teeming with the unwashed, the discarded, the forgotten. From time to time a piercing shriek would cut across the constant hum of moans and groans vibrating against the walls, and I would know that one more of these miserable

poor had been caught trying to escape. He would be fet-
tered to a bedpost like the other escapees, for the British maintained a well-ordered colony; there would be
no filthy indigents littering their streets. Once I had to
cut the toenails of an old man who was tied like that to
a bedpost, rope twisted around one of his legs. Urine
trailed down his pant leg, and yet, dutifully, believing I
was saving a soul, I clipped those nails that had grown
so long they curled upon themselves.

When my marriage failed I felt I was owed support
from the church to which I had given much of my youth.
I felt I had earned the church's love and understanding.
I had no family in America except for my brother David
who was enmeshed in marital problems of his own. My
parents and all my other siblings were either in Trinidad
or other parts of the world. I was angry with the church,
but I was desperate to belong, to attach myself to something familiar, something I had known from my past: a
community, a church that had been the center of my life
in my homeland. In desperation I sought out my parish
priest. I wanted him to tell me I could have a second
chance to fall in love, I could remarry, I could be happy.

Was I seeking an annulment? the priest wanted to
know. No, I said. I had been married for twenty years;
I had a son. My marriage contract was solid; I was perfectly aware of what I was doing when I made my vows.
My son was not born out of wedlock. What I wanted
was a divorce. What I wanted—it became distressingly
apparent to me—was the church's permission to divorce
my husband.

I could divorce my husband, the priest conceded,
but I could not remarry, for in the eyes of the church, the

man I had married would remain my husband until one of us died. To have sex with another man was to commit adultery, to break the sixth commandment. I would have to promise to be celibate for the rest of my life or risk eternal damnation. I was still young, still sexually in my prime. I could not make that promise.

A woman saved me, a nun dressed in civilian clothes. I was standing on the pavement in front of the rectory when she approached me. She must have seen the deadness in my eyes; she must have sensed my despair. "Is anything the matter? Can I help you?" Immediately a trembling began in my body. My lips quivered, my hands shook. She reached out and held me still. I leaned against her shoulder and poured out my heart to her. "It's a sin to stay in a marriage that is killing your spirit," she said. "Leave. Get a divorce."

She freed me. I wish I knew her name. I would thank her for removing the shackles of a religion that had imprisoned me.

When my divorce was final I couldn't wait to return to my maiden name. The day my lawyer confirmed I was single again, I strode into the HR office of my college employer and persuaded the director of personnel to change my surname immediately back to Nunez on all my official documents. She must have seen the urgency in my eyes, for my next paycheck was made out to Elizabeth Nunez. By this time all my anger and resentment toward D— had been drained out of me, so it wasn't that I wanted to erase his name; I just wanted mine back. I wanted to reclaim myself, the person I was before I married D—. I wanted back the life of my mind.

I was fifty when D— and I divorced. In the following

years I would rise in the ranks of the professoriate, ultimately achieving the title of Distinguished Professor. I would chair my academic department and for a year and a half I would be provost and senior vice president of my college. I had published one novel; I would publish seven more and several essays. I would travel around the country and abroad giving readings of my work. I would serve on literary panels and on juries for national and international prizes. I had no crystal ball to see that future when I got divorced, but I believed in its possibility with all my heart.

Sterner stuff? Had I inherited it too from my father who camouflaged his cautionary tale to his children with a joke about an English overseer and his brown-skinned sugarcane worker? *What done bile, done spile.* My father's admonitions served me well. I stiffened my back.

My son Jason was not happy, though, with my decision to reclaim my birth name. He was a young black man in America, struggling against racial stereotypes that attempted to define him. For his generation there was the War on Drugs, but the fuel Senator Daniel Moynihan gave to Lyndon Johnson's War on Poverty in the previous generation still lingered in the collective consciousness of the American people. Moynihan had made no attempt to sugarcoat his words. The title of his research, now referred to with the anodyne caption of *The Moynihan Report*, was originally *The Negro Family: The Case for National Action.* Single black mothers were to blame; absent black fathers were to blame, Moynihan contended. They were responsible for the bloated welfare rolls. It wasn't difficult for Jason's generation to connect the dots: households headed by single black mothers = poverty = drugs. Jason was starting college. He wanted us to have the same surname, the same one as his father. He wanted the world to know he was not a Moynihan statistic, that he came from an intact family, that he had a mother and a father who were married when he was born.

Surprisingly, Betty Shabazz, who at that time was an administrator at my college, also disapproved of my decision. "D— is a good man," she said to me. "What you are doing is an insult to him."

Betty Shabazz was Malcolm X's widow, the mother of their six daughters. I had great admiration for her, particularly for her devotion to the legacy of her husband. She was a tenacious advocate for ensuring Malcolm X's place as a crucial leader of the civil rights movement. But I disagreed with her. My ex may have been insulted by my decision to return to my maiden name, humiliated before his macho friends, but *my feelings* mattered more to me, and I believed deeply that I would be the one insulted if I kept his surname, if I made a mockery of all I had worked hard for, the years I had endured my grief in silence.

Now, as I watch my sisters reviewing the details of the High Mass that will be said for our mother, rejecting and selecting this or that prayer, this or that hymn, I feel the unspoken tension rippling through the room, I sense the dark cloud hovering above them. Most of my siblings have been divorced and have remarried. We are not celibate. What will we do when the bell rings for Communion at the High Mass my sisters are planning for our mother? Will we rise from our kneelers like the rest of the congregation and join the file of the faithful to the altar? All eyes will be on us, the eyes of our relatives, friends, neighbors, the merely curious. Will we bring dishonor to our mother's name, imply that she failed to raise us as good Catholics, if we do not also stand before the altar, our tongues outstretched to receive Communion? Everybody knows that the soul has to be free from sin to receive the body and blood of Christ.

16

I have blamed the church, but shall I blame my mother too? I have found reasons to explain her emotional distance from her children, but was she also responsible for not giving me the emotional nurturing I needed that would have made me less craving for love, less needy? Is it because of her that I find myself attracted to men equally incapable of allowing themselves tangible demonstrations of their love for me, incapable of open displays of affection?

Is it possible that my mother was stingy with her hugs and kisses because she did not love her children? Did not love me?

In my novel *Anna In-Between*, Anna Sinclair does not doubt that her mother, Beatrice Sinclair, loves her husband, though perhaps her husband loves Beatrice more. But Anna is not as confident that her mother loves *her*. After all, her mother sent her away, to America. She abandoned her. This is not her mother's truth; it is the truth as Anna sees it.

One year shy of forty, Anna continues to be plagued by feelings of abandonment. The source of pain is ancient, she tells us, but the feelings fresh, insistent. She blames her mother. "You've never asked me to come back," she grumbles. And her mother responds: "I've never asked you to come back because America can give you more than we can give you here. You have a big job in America . . . You wouldn't have a job like that if you stayed here."

In *Boundaries*, a novel that follows Anna's story, Anna has a big job, and more: She has fallen in love with a wonderful man. She has a chance now to create a family and a home in America. Still, she is pursued by the same feelings of abandonment. When her mother visits her in New York and expresses her delight that Anna has adjusted wonderfully in America, Anna lashes out at her: "Is that what you want, or is it what you see?" No sooner do these words leave her tongue than Anna is remorseful, ashamed of herself for striking out again at her mother. For the truth is that she *has* made a good life for herself in America. "She needs to let go," we are told. "She is too old to be holding on to childhood resentments."

I have never had such conversations with my mother. I would not have been able to withstand the pain in my mother's eyes, her guilt. Yes, like Beatrice Sinclair my mother would have said that she believed she was giving me a chance to take advantage of the opportunities America offered. But it happened that the year I graduated from secondary school was the very year Trinidad gained independence from Britain. We were no longer a colony, no longer governed by Britain. We had our own flag, our own national anthem; we could chart our own course. The University of the West Indies was no longer the University College of the West Indies, an arm of the University of London; it too was independent. And my family was not poor. By then, my father had an important position in the Shell Oil Company, and years before that he had risen quite high up the ranks of the colonial civil service. We had connections; there were opportunities for me in Trinidad. None of the usual reasons why immigrants leave their homelands held true for me. Yet my mother did everything she could to encourage not only me but also my siblings to leave the island.

The three of our eleven who remained in Trinidad seemed to have done so more by happenstance than by intention. Jacqueline married her childhood sweetheart and started a family in Trinidad; Karen, I believe, would have stayed abroad except for a difficult pregnancy in a marriage that was floundering; and Wally would be in England, Canada, or America had he been able to tolerate the colleges where my parents had sent him. As for my mother's claim that there would be more opportunities for us in America than there in Trinidad, that turned out to be false. Both my sisters and my brother have very comfortable lives in Trinidad, much more luxurious than my life in New York. My sisters drive expensive cars, they have huge homes with swimming pools, they entertain lavishly, they travel extensively, and they have held key positions in the private and public sectors. My brother runs a successful business.

I was amused when an angry colleague berated me for having the temerity to seek the position of chair of my academic department at Medgar Evers College, a predominantly black institution. "You can't come here on your banana boat and feel you can take what my people have suffered and died for," she said. "Our blood was spilled to get this college. Know your place. You'd be nothing back on your banana island. Be grateful!"

I sometimes think immigrants serve to reinforce the

sense Americans—both black and white—have of their country's superiority over other nations. Immigrants, after all, are the tired, the poor, the huddled masses, the wretched refuse—stereotypes etched in the collective consciousness of Americans from words engraved on that gift from the French. Americans seem to lap up stories that perpetuate the stereotype: needy immigrants, poor immigrants, downtrodden immigrants, uneducated immigrants. The other stories do not excite them as much: immigrants who are grateful, yes, but who credit their rise in the world to families they left behind, to a culture and a system of education that nurtured them.

So why was my mother so determined to send all her children abroad if there were opportunities for them on our oil-rich island? It cannot be possible that she didn't love us, or that we had become such a burden to her she wanted to get rid of us. My mother, I believe, was hostage to the social class to which fate had assigned her. She had fought her way out and was determined she was never going back to the indignities she had suffered. None of her children would. In the confines of our small island everyone knew your business, and your family's past became the yardstick to measure your future, but in the world outside her children would have a chance to make their own histories, to stretch their wings, to soar. She would send her children out into that world.

I know a lot about my father's family; I know almost nothing about my mother's. From my good friend Anne-Marie, whose father was the first local chief medical officer on the island, I learned that my maternal grandfather was a respected intellectual before he succumbed to alcoholism. I remember seeing him just once as he lay dying on his bed in a drunken stupor.

My mother loved her mother, Florence, but she was as secretive about her mother's past as she was about the rest of her family. All she would tell me was that Florence was one of the most beautiful women on the island. I have never seen a photograph of her, but I have heard stories. I do not know if these stories are true—my mother never confirmed their veracity—but they bring me closer to understanding my mother, her frantic obsession with keeping the door to her past shut and firmly bolted, the fear she must have suffered in silence that the past could seep out and stain her children's future. She would send us away, out of the island, to another country far across the ocean. She had to be strong; she had to guard her secrets.

I was told that Florence was the daughter of a poor black woman and a white Englishman who had taken advantage of her. Her mother sold fruits and vegetables in the open market and often took her daughter with her. One day an English couple spotted little Florence in the market and persuaded her mother to allow them to raise her child. What the English couple actually had in mind was a playmate for their daughter, who had no siblings. When the husband was reassigned to Grenada, the couple took Florence with them. They treated her kindly, gave her all the advantages their daughter had, but when they were recalled to England, they sent Florence back to her mother in Trinidad. She was a young teenager by then; she had known no other life but one of privilege. How could she go back to living in a hovel with a mother who was a common haggler in the street market? She was ashamed of her mother, ashamed of the life her mother lived. Soon she attracted the attentions of a wealthy man, but when she became pregnant by him, he abandoned her. My grandfather heard about Florence's troubles, and perhaps as a favor to her mother (I have no proof of this and perhaps no favor was necessary; Florence was beautiful), he married her though she was carrying another man's child. That child was my uncle Lex, my mother's stepbrother, who became a successful pharmacist. I met Lex a couple of times, always in his pharmacy, never in his home. I never met his wife. His children went to my secondary school; they never acknowledged me.

Skin color was another—and sure—route to upward mobility in Trinidad's colonial system. Lex's children were light-skinned; they were welcomed by the upper classes on the island. I was butterscotch brown, deep butterscotch brown.

These then are the stories I know about my mother's family: tales of Florence, my maternal grandmother, and Charles, her alcoholic husband; gossip about their children. There was also Cecil, a brother who was an upstanding citizen, but he died when I was in elementary school. My mother's only and younger sister, Eda, was my godmother, and when I was a child I grew very close to her. Eda had a child out of wedlock, and though this "indiscretion" disappointed my mother, she had forgiven Eda, hoping that one day her sister would redeem herself. She did not, not in my mother's eyes. My aunt fell in love and got married. Her husband turned out to be a gambler who plunged my aunt and the eight children they subsequently had into an unrelenting spiral of poverty. My mother continued to see her sister and to support her financially, but our families did not interact with each other. Today, I would not recognize my cousins if I bumped into them on the street.

When my mother married my father, she must have felt this was her chance to erase her past. She was now Una Nunez, but I believe she never lost her feelings of inadequacy. Deep down, I think she always felt as if she were an impostor, as if she did not, could not belong to the Nunez family. I think it was that feeling of insecurity that drove her to make certain that her children would be successful. She would join my father in his determination to instill in us that sterner stuff, even if it meant withholding tangible expressions of her love that she believed could weaken us, distract us, deter us from her goals for us. If not her, then her children would be true Nunezes.

At the time of my mother's marriage to my father, the Nunezes were one of the island's most distinguished families. They lived in a huge Victorian house, with white-fretted gables, at a major crossroad in Diego Martin. My grandfather had been a headmaster and a district warden. My father and all his sisters and brothers had graduated from the most established private secondary schools on the island. My eldest uncle was a pilot in the Royal Air Force and had become a hero when his bomber plane was shot down over Germany; my uncle Winston was a famous evangelical minister in Canada, passing as a white man; my aunt Lois, who like my uncle Winston had also inherited my grandmother's pale skin, seemed also to have fooled her white neighbors, for she was married to the mayor of Lancashire in England. My uncles Euan and John were on their way up the civil service ladder; one would become permanent secretary of housing, the other the permanent secretary of health. My uncle Mervyn, the youngest of my father's brothers, following his hero brother George, was a pilot in the Royal Air Force in England, and would eventually become a captain in the British Overseas Airline Company. My grandmother too was establishing her name as a grand dame of culture and the arts at the time my mother met my father. She played the piano and had a respectable singing voice. My grandfather used to play the violin and was a talented sculptor who used wood to create exquisite art objects, and I suppose he encouraged my grandmother when she began to take tentative steps toward turning her living room into a sort of Bloomsbury salon.

I have written an essay about my grandmother's salon that was published by the Folger Shakespeare Library in Washington, DC, for a chapbook celebrating the 2012 exhibition *Shakespeare's Sisters*. The title of the exhibition is a reference to Virginia Woolf's speculations in "A Room of One's Own" about the lives of women writers in Shakespeare's time. In my essay, I suggest that the salons that mushroomed in Trinidad in the 1950s were triggered by the tragic suicide of Virginia Woolf. My grandmother hosted one such salon, not with any sort of regularity, but, as was the custom in the Caribbean, people just dropped by. And what people!! It was there I met Beryl McBurnie, who, as I mentioned earlier, gave me permission to express my admiration for our local culture and reinforced an aesthetic undermined by the British colonizers. McBurnie was a great influence on my father's sister, my aunt Pearl, who was married to the celebrated opera singer, composer, and actor Edric Connor, who was raised in the coastal village of Mayaro, and with whom she created the first agency for artists of color in London. Edric was the first black actor to perform with the Royal Shakespeare Company in Stratford-upon-Avon, playing Gower in Shakespeare's *Pericles*. After he died, my aunt founded the Negro Theatre Workshop in London with her second husband, the musician and South African activist Joseph Mogotsi. My cousin Geraldine, the daughter of my aunt Pearl and my uncle Edric, was the creator of *Carnival Messiah*, the grand operatic musical theater hailed all over the world for its extraordinary costuming, staging, music, dance, and dramatic performances.

I met many other artists in my grandmother's salon who would influence my decision to become a writer: the Guyanese novelist Jan Carew; his Cuban-born wife Sylvia Wynter, a writer and literary critic; the Trinidadian Holder brothers, Boscoe and Geoffrey. Boscoe and his equally talented brother were choreographers, dancers, actors, pianists, and painters. Years later, not long before my mother died, I ran into Geoffrey Holder at Penn Station in New York. Ran into him is not accurate. I was on my way to Washington, DC, and one of my past students who was working for Amtrak's superfast train line, the Acela, spotted me and invited me to wait in the more comfortable Acela waiting room. I saw Geoffrey Holder before he noticed me, shocked that he did at all. I was a girl when my grandmother held sway over that gathering of artists in her drawing room. But there he was, calling out to me: "I know you." His voice boomed across the waiting room.

He was seated next to a tower of expensive boxed luggage, looking very much the movie star, a gorgeous taupe cape draped across his shoulders and falling elegantly down to his long legs. Heads already turned to stare at him now turned to stare at me. "Nunez. You must be a Nunez," he declared. "Waldo's daughter," I said. He wasn't sure of Waldo but he knew the Nunezes. "You have the Nunez face," he said, his theatrical voice coming from deep within his cavernous chest. He remembered my grandmother, remembered those gatherings in her drawing room. "What a grand dame!" And my aunt Pearl. "She kept her doors open for all of us struggling artists in London." But, of course, he was no longer a struggling artist. He had won two Tony Awards for stage direction and costume design for the Broadway production of *The Wiz*, and to a generation he will always be Punjab in the movie version of *Annie*. I also knew that he was a principal dancer at the Metropolitan Opera Ballet. His brother Boscoe was also a dancer. Boscoe had his own dance company that had performed at the coronation of Queen Elizabeth II in London. But what I know most about Boscoe is that he was a painter. Today his exquisite paintings can fetch hundreds of thousands of dollars.

There were so many others who spent long hours at my grandparents' house exchanging ideas, singing and dancing as my grandmother accompanied them on the piano. I owe my love for classical music and opera to these artists, but also to my father who played the violin in his youth and was a fan of Toscanini. The best presents I could bring back home for him after I immigrated to America were gramophone records, and, later, CDs of the music of the great composers. He, in exchange, would take me to the art galleries in Trinidad, where he was a familiar face and had already amassed an impressive collection of paintings.

Years later, as his work wound down when he was in his late seventies, my father renewed his friendship with the Goliahs, a brother and sister, both black Trinidadians who went to Germany after the Second World War, the brother, Schuler, to study medicine, the sister, Beatrice, mostly to accompany him, though she too went to university. Now, both retired, the Goliahs often visited my parents. My mother took a particular delight in Beatrice, who never married and was a bit of an eccentric. She was a wiry-thin, dark-brown woman, older than my mother, a woman my mother believed would in no way attract the attentions of my father. Except she did. For my father found Beatrice interesting too, not for her eccentricity, but for her love of music. Soon he was visiting the Goliahs without my mother. Sometimes on my trips to Trinidad, he would take me with him, and while Schuler puttered around in his rooms, my father and Beatrice would sit together sipping port, legs stretched out, while German lieders played on an ancient record player.

So how was my mother to compete? How could she set the mess of her family background against the stability and grandeur of the talented Nunezes? My mother's ambition for herself became her ambition for her children. We were programmed to succeed; we had no other choice. Before we reached the starting gate, our mother prepared us. She taught us to read, write, and do simple arithmetic. From our first day in school we were already ahead of all the other children, and my mother made certain we remained there. To come second in class was not good enough. We had to be first. I was reading by the time I was three years old; my brother David was so prepared that he was barely ten when he won a scholarship to the prestigious St. Mary's College secondary school.

My mother's aim seemed to be to prove to her mother-in-law, Georgiana Nunez, that her daughters too could go to St. Joseph's Convent, the secondary school my paternal aunts attended, and her sons would go to St. Mary's College like my paternal uncles. Yet my mother wanted more. Her in-laws had all traveled abroad when they were young adults. She wanted us to go abroad too; she wanted us to have a university education in the big countries. The umbilical cord that bound us to her was cut when we were born. She cut her apron strings if we held on too long. My older sister was dry-eyed when the ship carrying her to England left the dock, though she knew it would be years before she would see us or her homeland again. I too was dry-eyed when, at nineteen, I left my warm and sunny island for the frigid landscapes of Wisconsin where I knew no one.

I try to put my mother's reasoning in perspective. The mother bird fails if her babies remain in the nest. She succeeds when they fly away on their own. Yet it seems to me that my mother was driven by a more pressing goal. She needed to prove to the Nunezes that her blood, tainted as she assumed they thought it was, could produce doctors, lawyers, engineers, professors, mathematicians. She would show them. So she sent us away; she pushed us out of our home. And in the end, didn't her gamble pay off?

In *Anna In-Between*, Anna Sinclair chokes with resentment over the pleasure her mother takes in her success. For years she has allowed her mother to believe that she is a major player in one of the most important publishing houses in New York. The truth is that she is merely the head of a small imprint within that publishing house. Her anger toward her mother is unremitting: "You wanted me to lie to you. I am important to you because of what you can boast to your friends about me. Not because of me. I am a trophy for you to put on your shelf, to dust off when you are entertaining your friends."

Anna must find a way to release herself from her resentment before it destroys her future.

I faced the same predicament.

17

There is the wake. Except for one of us, whose absence still baffles me to this day, we are all there, my father and ten of his children. Chairs are placed in a semicircle a short distance from my mother's coffin, which is raised on a dais. Against the back wall, at the opposite end of the room, is a comfortable overstuffed couch. My father stands in front of it, his shoulders caved in. He looks drained, exhausted. He takes a step forward and I think he means to sink himself into the couch. I am wrong; he totters for a second, almost losing his balance, but then he straightens up. I notice the return of the twitching around his temples, though, the fluttering I saw the day I arrived. It is barely perceptible, and at first I think nothing of it, but then the twitching increases, snaking down his arms and legs in tiny rolling waves. Soon he begins to drum his fingers against his thighs, his fingers moving faster and faster, pressing the fabric of his pant legs into his flesh. His eyes stretch open wide and a vacuous grin parts his thin lips. I nudge one of my brothers. "Go to him," I say.

Two of my brothers approach my father, but now he is no longer standing still. He is dancing. It is a strange dance and we stare at him in astonishment. He stomps one foot on the ground and then the other, each time his body shaking rhythmically to a beat he alone hears. Inch by inch he moves forward, the dance taking him toward the front of the room where my mother lies stiff and still in her coffin. The image of scantily dressed Africans in a village ceremony dancing to the beat of tribal drums flashes across my mind. I chase the image away. This is my father, the collector of fine art, the lover of classical music, the man who quotes Shakespeare to me, the man who oversaw billions of dollars for an international oil company. But my father is dancing faster now, the grin on his face full blown into soundless laughter, his eyes darting mischievously across the room, not directed toward us, not at my mother's still body either, but at something in the far unseen distance, something that fills him with joy.

And suddenly a curtain parts, and I know what he sees; I know what he hears. It is not the dancers he sees—hip-writhing, bare-breasted women in an ancient village ceremony—nor does he hear the thrum and boom of African drums. It is the color-splashed Carnival of his days and mine that glitters before his eyes; it is the music of the streets, the heart-pounding rhythms of the steel pan that pulsate through his ears.

On the last day of our two-day Carnival, just as the sun was beginning to set, my father would take his daughters and wife for a last lap, a jump-up with him through the city streets. How we had waited for that moment! For two days my brothers were free to follow the bands, but my sisters and I were forced to stay with our mother and the younger children on the sidewalk of the car park behind my father's office. He would check on us from time to time, but mostly he was gone, jumping up with his friends in the Carnival bands.

Is this the memory that travels through my father's head now, filling him with joy, with remembrances of mischief? Is he recalling those late Carnival afternoons when he slipped back to us, his face alive with the beat of the steel pan music pulsating through his ears? As darkness began to fall, he would return from the company of his friends, teasing a smile on his wife's face, enclosing her in his wide arms, and we, his daughters, relieved to see them happy together, would press our faces against them.

How we danced and danced through the streets of our city, hands waving in the air, feet slapping against the asphalt cooled in the evening breeze, the heat of the day swept away with the descending sun, the sky a canopy of bright stars above us! Our mother was young again, in love again, her head flung back against her husband's shoulders, her arm encircling his waist.

But now, as my father comes closer to my mother's coffin, he slows down. He slides one foot forward and then the other, all energy seemingly drained from his legs. My brothers tighten their hold on his elbows. They have reached the edge of the dais, and the wide smile that seconds ago broke across my father's face has disappeared completely. His lips form a tight, thin line, his chest caves in, his head lolls to one side on his neck. One of my brothers whispers something in his ear, and my father looks down on my mother's frozen face. The dull, empty expression that was in his eyes when he first entered the room returns, but even duller now, lifeless. He does not resist when my brothers lead him away to the couch in the back of the room. He slumps down on the cushioned seat and closes his eyes. Mercifully, he falls asleep.

Jacqueline says we should pray the rosary. It was our mother's favorite prayer. We sit on the semicircle of chairs. Jacqueline chooses the Glorious Mystery. There are five parts to this mystery: the first, the Resurrection of Christ; the second, the Ascension of Christ into heaven; the third, the Descent of the Holy Spirit; the fourth, the Assumption of Mary; the fifth, the Coronation of the Blessed Virgin. As Jacqueline calls out each section of the Glorious Mystery, it becomes clear to me why, of all the mysteries of the rosary, this was my mother's favorite. The Assumption of Mary: not only did Christ rise from the dead, but His mother too ascended, body and soul, into heaven.

My mother loved Mary. The mother of God was a comfort to her. She had lost her mother not long after the birth of her second child. I was two; my brother was one, my mother likely pregnant again. My mother needed a mother; she turned to the mother of God.

I too needed a mother when I had my son, alone in America, without family or friends to support me, my husband itching to return to his lover. But I did not have my mother's faith to call on the mother of Christ for comfort. Now, though, I find myself praying that Mary has not abandoned my mother. *Holy Mary, mother of God, pray for us sinners now and at the hour of our death.*

18

I have never seen my father cry. I did not expect to see him cry when he looked down on the body of the woman he had loved for sixty-five years. He told me he had cried only once in his life—except of course when he was a child and hurt himself or someone else hurt him. But since he became a man there was only one time he had allowed himself to yield to the pressure that sometimes built up behind his eyes when he was sad. My grandfather had just turned eighty and my father was cutting his hair, as he usually did once a month. Suddenly it struck him that his father would not have long to live. He said he broke down. He said he could not hold back his tears.

My father adored his father. His father was the sort of man my father aspired to be. I do not mean that my father wanted to be a district warden or a headmaster like my grandfather; I mean he aspired to be the kind of man who was capable of appreciating and enjoying both man's achievements and God's creations. My grandfather was a humanist, a true Renaissance man. He painted, he sculpted, he played the piano and violin; he taught himself ancient Greek and Latin; he hunted, fished, and was nearly unbeatable in chess as well as on the cricket mound. My father inherited most of his father's qualities. He too was a humanist, and a sort of

Renaissance man. He hunted, he fished, was a master at chess (though not at cricket), and an admirer of the arts and nature, but I never heard him play a musical instrument—though I knew he played the violin in his youth—or saw anything he sculpted or painted, and as far as I know his reading was limited to P.G. Wodehouse and the newspapers, especially the comics.

I knew my grandfather fairly well, for my father took us often to visit him, generally once or twice a week. Though my father despaired that at eighty my grandfather would soon be taken away from him, my grandfather in fact lived many more years, his mind sharp when he declared he'd had enough and days later lay down on his bed and died, two years shy of his hundredth birthday. In that last year he was frequently in pain, but the year before he was still vigorous, climbing the pommerac tree in his backyard and feeding the stray dogs that came to his door. He was in his nineties when he helped me with my doctoral dissertation that was partly based on *The Tempest*.

I was trying to make sense of Trinculo's scornful description of Caliban:

A fish: he smells like a fish; a very ancient and fishlike smell; a kind of not of the newest Poor John [dried, salted fish]. A strange fish!

"Why like a fish?" I asked. "Was it because Caliban ate fish?"

"Oh no," said my grandfather. "He was probably someone like a Warao."

My grandfather used to trade goods with the Waraos

in the open market in the forests, not far from the middle of the south coast of Trinidad. He was a young man then, not yet married to my grandmother. The Waraos would come over on their pirogues from Venezuela, place their goods—mainly fruits and vegetables—in the middle of the clearing used for the market, and then hide in the bushes. My grandfather and his neighbors would take the food and in exchange leave clothes, utensils, and trinkets for the Waraos.

"Even though we couldn't see them," my grandfather explained, "we could smell them. I wouldn't say they stank. But they did have a very strong scent of fish." He told me that the Waraos covered themselves from head to foot with fish oil to ward off mosquitoes and other insects that brought disease. "Very clever, but you wouldn't want to get too close to them even if they would let you. The smell was pungent." That story so fired my imagination that it found its way into my first novel.

But though my father admired my grandfather for his love of nature and the arts, I think he was especially close to him because they shared physical features that made them both outsiders in their social class. My grandfather, like my father, was dark-skinned, the color of a ripened cocoa pod. Genes from his pale-skinned Portuguese father were not strong enough to lessen the intensity of the melanin he inherited from his African mother. I was told that he changed his surname from Nunes to Nunez because of his outrage over the refusal of the colonial government to add a footnote to the books schoolchildren used, explaining Keats's error in his poem, but my father told me another story. He said that the light-skinned Portuguese community had disassociated itself from my dark-skinned grandfather, so he in turn disassociated himself from them. "Anyhow," my father added scornfully, "they were shopkeepers. My father was a headmaster." Be that as it may, my father's older brother Winston saw value in capitalizing on his Portuguese surname, Nunes, when he chose to pass for white as an evangelical minister in Canada.

My grandfather's brother also kept Nunes as his last name. He was pale-skinned, but when he immigrated to America, he discovered that one drop (and he had many more than one drop) was all that was needed to make you a Negro. In America, even in so-called liberal New York, Negroes were corralled in specific places. My great-uncle lived in Harlem. He became a successful dentist, but without family in America to take care of him in his old age, he ended up in the nursing home at Harlem Hospital. He died a pauper, all his holdings, magnificent houses on Strivers' Row, appropriated by the hospital to pay for his boarding and medical fees.

Only one of my father's siblings, a younger brother whom my father outlived, was as dark as he, and I would hazard to guess that he, like my father, had felt the brunt of color discrimination on the island. I say my mother's ambitions for us were motivated by her insecurity, but my father was insecure too. My mother was driven to prove to the Nunezes that she could produce brilliant and successful children. My father was driven to prove to his family that even a dark-skinned Nunez could produce brilliant and successful children.

My father told me stories of the beatings he endured from his schoolmasters at St. Mary's College. Not only he, but my grandmother too, believed the Jesuits picked on him because he was dark-skinned. Neither of her older sons, my father's two light-skinned brothers, was beaten as viciously or as frequently as my father was. He was beaten for the smallest infractions—say, for mispronouncing a Latin word, making an error in his mathematics homework, or arriving late for school after having to wake up before dawn to tie up the cow that was the source of income for his school fees. Would that the Jesuits could have seen my father at the height of his career! Of all his siblings, my father was the most successful—and I daresay of all his classmates as well.

Trinidadians are fond of claiming that the island has fortunately escaped the scourge of racism that continues to plague America. It is a myth that keeps Trinidadians from looking too deeply into that mirror where the face of the colonizer could be reflected back as their own. My brother Richard tells me that only in America is he conscious of his skin color. He says that from the moment he crosses the threshold of an airport in America, he realizes, as if for the first time, his difference from whites. This is the same brother who says he was spurned by the family of his biological mother because his skin was darker than his sister's. His sister, like her French Creole mother, is light-skinned and my brother is convinced that this is the reason she was often invited to spend holidays with their French Creole family, he very rarely. To this day, now a grandfather, Richard continues to retell this story. Still, though this experience burns in his chest, he insists that discrimination in Trinidad, where it exists (and for him it rarely exists), is based on class rather than color.

How that distinction soothes the souls of so many Trinidadians who disavow their darker and, as inevitably it turns out, their poor relatives! For as if it remains an unsolvable mystery to them, too many Trinidadians claim not to see the observable reality that, with rare exceptions, the shades of skin color of the upper class in Trinidad, often the moneyed class, run from European pale-beige to café au lait. The darker the skin color, the more likely it is that the person is poor or from the working class. And why not? Color was valuable currency in the colonies; it could help make you rich or poor, working class or upper class.

So did my father marry the French Creole mother of my older brother and sister in part because she was light-skinned? Was he thinking that if his children inherited their mother's light skin, more doors would be open to them than were open to him when he was growing up?

At the end of his wildly popular book *Outliers*, Malcolm Gladwell turns to his family. For most of the book he has focused on supporting his thesis that social environment, the influence of parents, and the historical events that occur during a person's childhood are fundamental to the shaping of the outlier. Now, giving us a window to the success of his mother's family in Jamaica, he adds another factor. He tells us that his great-great-great-grandfather, William Ford, was Irish. He had a son, John Ford, with an Igbo tribeswoman from West Africa, and from that moment began "the privilege of a skin color" his mother's family enjoyed as colored Jamaicans on an island where people benefited for generations on a hierarchy based on the shade of their skin.

"The brown-skinned classes of Jamaica came to fetishize their lightness," Gladwell adds. "It was their great advantage."

I have no proof that my father was thinking about the advantages of a French Creole mother for his children when he first married. What I know is that my mother's brown skin had not mattered to him. When he thought of having children with my mother, it was Mendel's experiments with pea plants—which were being applied to all sorts of living organisms, reaching their diabolical apotheosis in Hitler's gruesome experiments—that had given him pause and caused him, in 1942, to consult a physician, who, like other physicians at that time in Trinidad, did double duty as a psychiatrist. Ironically, though, it would be my father whose intellectual capacity would deteriorate. Until her last hour, in spite of a stroke, my mother's mind remained as sharp as a tack. But my father's hesitation to marry my mother did not last long, for he had fallen deeply and irretrievably in love with her. It was a passion that would endure, increasing, not lessening, through the years.

I know, though, that my father was humiliated because of his skin color. He never forgot those beatings he got from the Jesuits, but the story he often repeated to me, because it was the incident that hurt him the most, was about feeling like an outsider within his own family.

He is a young man, twenty or twenty-one, in his first job in the colonial civil service. He has stayed after work in the city to have drinks with friends. It is dark when he and his friends part, and my father takes the bus home to Diego Martin. He sits in the back. It is a long trip from Port of Spain to Diego Martin and he is tired and slightly tipsy. Soon he dozes off. He does not hear when passengers get on or off the bus, but suddenly he is awakened by the sounds of raucous laughter. A group of young women and men are sitting not far in front of him. The men are telling jokes that send the women into fits of laughter. The women are beautiful, the men are beautiful, all of them beautifully dressed. They are going to a party. He knows this because they talk about the people they expect to see there. They name names. The people they name are people from Trinidad's upper-middle-class families, people like them, light-skinned, with straight or curly hair. They talk about who is going to play the piano, who is going to sing. These are the days before the gramophone reached most of the homes in colonial Trinidad. Music is live and most cultured young ladies and gentlemen are expected to have some fundamental knowledge of a musical instrument, or at least know how to hold a tune. They tease each other: who is the better piano player, who stinks at the violin, who sings off-key. Through the bursts of laughter and the animated conversation, three words slip out and galvanize my father's attention: *Diego Martin. Nunez.*

"They were going to Diego Martin," he tells me. "To the Nunezes. They were talking about my sisters: Lois, Ethyne, Jean, Pearl. One of the women turns and sees me staring at them. I think I was about to say something about it being my home where they were going, that Lois, Ethyne, Jean, and Pearl are my sisters, but before the words could leave my mouth, the woman wags her finger at me. *What are you looking at, you silly boy? Mind your own business. Don't you have friends in your own backwater village?* Her friends hooted and howled with laughter. I slunk back down in my seat. These were people who had simply judged me by the color of my skin. I was coming from work so I was dressed in suit and tie, just like the young men in their group, but it was my dark skin that told them I was not of their class, not fit to be in their company."

I was aghast when my father first told me this story, though I shouldn't have been. Shouldn't have been because I know our history. In 1829, mulattoes are freed. Five years later, in 1834, the Emancipation Act takes effect, but it is nine years in all before the enslaved Africans get their freedom in 1838. *Chattel slavery is now wage slavery!* the Africans had thundered through the streets when the British called for a transition of six years after the Emancipation Act—a needed period of apprenticeship, they claimed. The victory the Africans won was limited; not six years, but four before enforced "wage slavery" finally came to an end.

I have read Lawrence Scott's remarkable novel *Light Falling on Bamboo*. He tells of the mulatto mother of the great Trinidadian painter Michel Jean Cazabon. She is forced to sit in the area for *gens de couleur*, far apart from the seats reserved for the *grands blancs* on the steamer that shuttles passengers back and forth from the south to the north of the island, but nowhere near where blacks are crammed in tight spaces below the deck. It was decades later when my father boarded that bus from Port of Spain to Diego Martin, but little had changed. He was still expected to know his place in the crammed quarters below the deck.

The humiliation my father suffered that evening had so affected him that it has shadowed him his whole life.

He took over where my mother left off. She prepared us for primary school; he made certain we would get into the best secondary schools and then to university to become doctors, lawyers, engineers, professions that had been virtually closed to dark-skinned men like him. His sons would have the credentials to compete with any Englishman. He did not get involved in their schoolwork—he relied totally on their teachers—but if their weekly scores were poor, he doled out the punishment, though not as severe as the beatings he had suffered from the hands of his Jesuit schoolmasters.

My father never struck his daughters, though; it was a principle of his that men should never strike a woman. Women were after all the weaker sex, and given this line of thinking, he did not expect as much from us as he did from his sons. His daughters were not groomed to be doctors, lawyers, and engineers. He wanted us to be educated as a sort of insurance against an unfortunate marriage. He had seen what happened to women who were trapped in marriages for financial reasons. He did not want us to suffer the same fate. As the women's movement gained traction, however, he was quick to change with the times. He deeply regretted he had not encouraged my older sister to become a physician. She was an excellent nurse, often selected by doctors to assist them in the operating theater. David loved working with her. He said she had the hands and nerves of a surgeon. My father did not make the same mistake with his two younger daughters: Karen he pretty much pushed into law; Judith he supported enthusiastically when she followed my older brother, becoming one of the few local actuaries in the Eastern Caribbean.

Our mother urged us to stay in our marriages because we had sworn an oath before God. Our father kept
his opinion to himself, but he was the first to invite his
daughters back home when our marriages became troubled. Twice he helped Jacqueline pack when she decided
to leave her husband, taking her two children with her,
and twice he helped her pack again when she returned
to her husband. When I finally decided to get a divorce,
my father supported me while my mother kept hoping
and praying for a reconciliation even after papers were
signed.

Jacqueline, who with Mary is the darkest of my sisters, tells me she was just twelve when our father set her
expectations for the treatment he believed she deserved
from any man who claimed to love her. One morning he
roused her out of her bed and announced that he and
our mother were taking her on a trip to Port of Spain.
They did not tell her why or where they would be going, only that she should put on her best clothes. At the
time our family was living in Point Fortin, in the south
of Trinidad, many miles from Port of Spain in the north.
The trip could take as many as two hours or more one
way, for the roads were winding and potholed in many
places. Generally we would spend the night when we
went to Port of Spain, but my parents told Jacqueline
they planned to return that same day.

As they wound their way along the mountain that
sloped down to the city, Jacqueline could see the roof-
top of the newly constructed Hilton Hotel—the upside-
down hotel we called it, for the entrance was at the top
of the hill, the rooms below. My father pulled into the
driveway of the Hilton and solved the mystery of the

early-morning trip. "There," he said to Jacqueline. "Your mother and I wanted to take you to tea at the Hilton so you could know the life you deserve."

Very early in Salman Rushdie's novel *Midnight's Children*, the narrator tells us that his mother's "dark skin stood between her and the affections of her mother," who was unable to love her daughter, Mumtaz, "the blackie," because of "her skin of a South Indian fisherwoman." Though she is anxious to have her daughters married to men whose social and financial positions would improve the family's status, the mother (she is referred to as the Reverend Mother) does not object to Mumtaz's marriage to the penniless "lank-haired, overweight" Nadir Khan whose political positions have forced him into hiding with the flying cockroaches in the dark space below her drawing room floor. Mumtaz, the "blackie," is lucky to have found someone willing to marry her.

At the wake for my mother, after the prayers have ended, I go with Jacqueline to wake my father who is still sound asleep on the couch in the back of the funeral parlor. Suddenly I find myself thinking of the unfortunate Mumtaz, of the time too when my father had taken Jacqueline for tea at the Hilton, his heart swelling with grief and fear for his young dark-skinned daughter. I think about my dark-skinned grandfather. Had he protected my father in the same way? Is that why my father had loved him so?

That's that, my father said as he walked away from my mother's coffin. He would have to live in the world without his wife and nothing he could do would change that fact. But at the wake his body betrayed him. It trembled;

it twitched; it swayed; it took him jumping up behind a steel pan band, his arm around the waist of his wife, his children pressed against him.

19

Did my mother love my father as much as he loved her? Did she love him at all? Or did she marry him, as I imagine her mother married my maternal grandfather, for financial support, trusting he would take care of her?

It is 1949. I have five siblings. There are six of us in all: Yolande, who is nine; Richard, who is eight; me, Elizabeth, who is five; David, who is four; Jacqueline, who is three; and Wally, who is the baby, not yet two. My father has been sent by the Ministry of Labour of the Trinidad and Tobago colonial government for training in London. He has left us with our mother. He has been gone six weeks, three of them on the ship that took him to England. We expect he will be in London for months. We have received many letters from him. After his first week in London, the letters seem to come almost daily in thin blue letter forms that are folded and glued at the top and sides, the way my paycheck arrives today, except the paper for my paycheck and paystub is stiffer and harder than the blue letter form which rips easily and has to be handled carefully or we could lose much of what has been written on it. We get postcards too, but the postcards are for us, the children. The letters are for my mother. She reads parts of them to us. My father writes about what he is doing, where he has been, who he has met. Inevitably, before she gets to the end, my mother begins to cry. Long tears roll down her cheeks, and she runs to the bedroom and shuts the door. We hear her sobbing through the thin walls.

One day I see her sitting near the window. My baby brother is on her lap but she seems hardly aware she is holding him. She is staring out of the window, into blank space, it seems to me. Soon her arms around my baby brother slacken and I fear he is about to fall. My mother does nothing to restrain him, her gaze remaining fixed outside of the room, her mind seeming to drift inward. My brother squirms and leans over her loosened arms. I reach over quickly and manage to save him just as he is about to fall and strike his head against the hardwood floor. He screams, startling my mother. Tears burst from her eyes. She mumbles something to me, something indecipherable, shoves my brother into my arms, and runs to her room.

Days pass. My mother hardly touches her food; she pays little or no attention to us. We have a live-in maid, Ena, who is happy to work for us because times are hard in a colony of a country that has suffered through two world wars in twenty-five years. When food is scarce in England, food is scarce on our island too; when the English people must use ration cards, we must use ration cards too; when they have no jobs, we have no jobs too; when they have no place to live, we have no place to live too. So though my parents pay Ena very little, she is grateful to be assured a bed and three square meals a day.

Ena and nine-year-old Yolande take charge. They make the meals, they feed the little ones, they bathe us, they put us to sleep. My mother helps too, but she does so in a trance, cooking sometimes, feeding the little ones sometimes, dressing us sometimes. For the most part, she cannot be relied upon. For the most part, she sits at the window reading my father's letters and afterward staring into space. When she stands up, her cheeks are wet.

One day she announces she is going to London. She will have to travel by ship across the Atlantic to get there. Three weeks the trip will take. It is August, hurricane weather in the tropics, summer in the northern countries, storms very likely. My mother is warned: there could be roiling seas, mountainous waves, thunder and lightning. Even the hardiest of travelers get sick at this time of the year. My mother is terrified of the sea; she is even more afraid of being alone in a cabin at sea, but she is not dissuaded. She will take Yolande with her for company, she says. They go together to the passport office in Port of Spain.

Who will take care of us? I do not know if I asked that question aloud, but I am sure it was foremost on my five-year-old mind.

At the last minute, my mother changes her plans. She won't take my sister with her. She will go to London without her. She wants to have her husband to herself when she gets there; there'll be years yet to share him with their children.

What will happen to us?

My mother makes an arrangement with her good friend Anne-Marie, who is single and has no children. Anne-Marie will come every evening after work to the house to make sure the older ones have been to school, that all of us have eaten, that we have showered, said our prayers, and are tucked into bed. During the day, Ena will take care of us. Dr. Joseph, our parents' friend and our family doctor, will check on us every weekend. If any of us get sick, Ena will call Dr. Joseph.

My mother leaves. Now we get postcards signed by the two of them. We get photographs too. At first our parents are wearing clothes we recognize. Our mother is in light cotton dresses, our father in short-sleeved shirts, but soon their clothes change. They are wearing sweaters. *And my mother has on pants!* I have never before seen my mother in pants. The fabric of the pants they are wearing is thick; it does not flap against their legs as my father's pants used to do. Behind them the leaves on the trees hang dry and wrinkled on their stems. Some have fallen and are clustered in small mounds near our parents' feet. Weeks pass and now our parents are bundled up in long heavy coats and thick scarves wrapped around their necks. They are wearing high boots, not shoes. "It was summer, then autumn, but now it's winter in London," Yolande explains to me—I have known only our two-season tropical weather, the wet and the dry.

Our parents do not neglect our education. They pose by monuments in London and write notes explaining the historical significance of each statue and pillar they see. In one photograph, which today hangs on a wall in my house, and on a wall in each of my sisters' homes, our parents are arm in arm in front of the fountain in Trafalgar Square, broad smiles on their faces. "Our darling children," the letter begins. Then we learn about Admiral Horatio Lord Nelson and his victory over the combined forces of the French and Spanish navies under Napoleon Bonaparte.

It is the end of the 1940s, and in England people are celebrating. World War II is over, London is rebuilding, people are gay again. Our parents are gay again. No squealing babies to interrupt their lovemaking. My mother especially is gay again. No babies to feed, no clothes to wash, no food to cook. She and our father are having the time of their lives. They take the ferry to France. In Paris they go to the clubs. Our father writes that our mother hid her face when the girls did the cancan at the Moulin Rouge at Place Pigalle.

How are they able to afford this lifestyle? They live in bed-sitters; they share the kitchen and bathroom with strangers. They don't mind. My father has a fellowship; it is enough to support his family, though not in any grand style. In Trinidad, we live in half of a rented house. Ena is glad to have meals every day, a place to sleep, and a salary that keeps her off the streets. Dr. Joseph does not charge us for his house calls.

Did I resent my parents for abandoning us? For that is what they did for months. I remember missing them, crying myself to sleep. I remember having to grow up suddenly when my younger siblings got measles and then all of us got the chicken pox. I remember that at five years old I had to put aside my own discomfort to take care of two toddlers and a child who had just learned to walk.

Do I resent them now? I look back and realize how young they were. My mother was thirty-one, my father thirty-five. They were in love, having the time of their lives.

Life is short. I'm glad they had this time together. I am glad to know that my mother was as passionately in love with my father as he was with her. And we survived.

Mary, our parents' seventh child, is glad to know she was conceived in this blissful period of carefree love, though in giving his sixth child his own name—Waldo—my father had hopes that he would be the last my mother would bear.

20

Did my mother's passion for my father last? Did it endure through the years, through the ups and downs of their sometimes tumultuous marriage, my father's infidelities?

I am chosen to write my mother's eulogy. What shall I write? My brothers and sisters gather around me and give me facts. Our mother was an upstanding member of her community, a pillar of her church, charitable to a fault with her time and money to those in need. She was an avid bridge player, the president of the Horticultural Society, admired and loved by her neighbors. Her children loved her. Her husband adored her.

I write and write, the good amanuensis, taking notes from my siblings but all the time battling a darkening fog gathering in my head. *Did my mother continue to love my father as he continued to love her, even more through the years? Did she forgive him for his infidelities?* Then, later, when I am alone, faced with the task of fashioning the notes into readable prose, the fog clears. I have remembered an afternoon in 2007, the year before my mother died.

I am on holiday from New York. It is late morning, an hour or so before lunch. The sun is making its ascent to the middle of the sky. In a very short time it will scorch the grass and burn the petals on the roses that line the walkway. Some will wither and die; some will fold into themselves and bloom again when the sun moves on. The birds are searching for shade in the cups of branches hidden behind a canopy of leaves. I hear the flutter of wings, the drone of flying insects. Then all is quiet outside. Inside the house, my mother is in her bedroom, saying her midmorning prayers. The TV is on, tuned to a religious channel. A priest leads the rosary and my mother joins the congregation, responding to the second half of each Hail Mary. Petra is in the kitchen. I hear the banging of pots and pans, the loud thud of the meat cleaver against the cutting board as she breaks through the bones of the meat we will have for lunch.

My father is in the backyard, occupying himself with his favorite pastime. He is picking up leaves that have fallen from the fruit trees. He does not have to do this. My parents employ a gardener. If the gardener needs help, they can afford to hire extra men. But my father likes being in the garden. He does not have much interest in the flowers; it's my mother who is the horticultural-ist. My father likes the big trees. I think they remind him of his youthful days in the forest, though the trees in their yard are surrounded by skirts of pristine lawn. Still, leaves and rotted fruit fall from big trees at unpre-dictable times, times when the gardener is not there or before my mother can call for additional help. So every morning, after breakfast, my father gathers the oranges and limes on the ground near their bedroom window. He walks over to the spreading sapodilla tree that shades the nursery, where my mother supervises the planting of seedlings and tends to the shoots of the most delicate flowers, and he picks up the rotting sapodillas, already pockmarked by birds in their early-morning feast. He throws them in the ravine behind the wall at the side of the house and moves on to the mango tree. He is ninety-two, skinny as a lamp pole, the muscles on his thighs and legs taut as wires. He is descending into dementia, willed, my mother insists; but if willed—if it is possible to will dementia—the habit of withdrawing from the world is beginning to solidify in him. Yet when he reaches the mango trees—one tree, it seems, until you taste the fruit—he calls out to me. "Elizabeth, which do you want, the sweet or the juicy?"

Many years ago, when I expressed surprise that one tree would bear two kinds of mangoes, a small, sweet mango starch and another larger, seemingly different kind, my father explained: "It's not one mango tree, but two, you see. And both are the same kind. Both are mango starch."

Originally both trees grew just a few feet from each other, then one got diseased so my father had it chopped down, but in the next rainy season it sprouted shoots that grew thicker and taller each year until its leafy branches wound themselves so tightly around the older and sturdier tree that it was difficult to tell where one began and the other ended.

A metaphor for my parents' love for each other? "I guess it does look like one tree," my father had conceded, and then added enigmatically, "but, of course, the mangoes are different."

A metaphor for the children he and my mother produced? Both mangoes were sweet, but the pulp in the smaller one was denser, the effect of the sweetness in the mouth immediate. The larger one demanded more,

more time, more effort—two or three mouthfuls—but its sweetness was just as intense.

My father handed me a mango. It was the small, sweet one. I am the shortest of their children. *Am I also the sweetest, the most loved?* I hardly got the chance to savor my victory when my father bent down again and gave me another. It was the larger, juicier one. "I like this one too," he said.

Now, on my way to the covered veranda with a book in my hand that I plan to read before lunch, I tell him that I will have both kinds, the sweet and the juicy, but for dessert, after lunch. He waves to me and resumes his morning work. He bends down, collects a few dried mango leaves, straightens up, puts them in a pile, and starts the process all over again. His younger sister Jean, who lives in England with her well-to-do English husband, is in Trinidad on holiday. She came to the house the day before, and seeing my father at his daily task was awestruck. "I am fifteen years his junior," she said, her mouth slack-jawed with admiration, "and if I tried to do that all that bending and rising that Waldo does, I'd be unable to get out of bed the next day."

In the veranda, I stretch out on a chaise lounge. My book slips to my lap. I am lulled by the deepening heat and the midmorning sounds drifting off to a comforting silence. I am drowsy. Soon I fall asleep. In minutes, though, I am awakened by urgent shouts. "Mr. Nunez! Mr. Nunez, wake up! Dr. Elizabeth! Mrs. Nunez! Something happen to Mr. Nunez! Come out quick! Come quick!"

I fly out of my chair and rush to the backyard. My father is slumped down on the bench under the mango tree. Petra is holding him up. Her arm is around his shoulders. By the time I reach them, she has managed to get my father on his feet. He wobbles a bit and smiles weakly at me. I tuck my arm in the crook of his elbow; Petra does the same on the other side.

"What happened, Daddy?" I ask. "Are you okay?"

He nods and makes an effort to steady his feet.

Petra tightens her grip. "I take you, Mr. Nunez," she says. She seems to know where, to know what he wants. She signals to me to move forward and I follow her lead.

My mother has not noticed the commotion outside, but she hears when we open the bedroom door, and when she sees her husband, walking more upright now, though Petra and I still have our arms locked around his elbows, she rushes toward us and we release him to her. Holding my father by his hand, my mother takes him to the armchair on her side of the bed. My habitual irritation at her kicks in: *Why not to his armchair, on his side of the bed? You know he'll be more comfortable there.* I almost say these words, but something holds me back, something I cannot name or explain. A feeling. I am not wanted here. These are my parents but at this moment they are husband and wife. They do not need me. My father does not need me to defend him. My mother knows what he wants.

I go to the bathroom, and fill a glass with water, and bring it to my father. He drinks. Little by little his shoulders rise from where they were sunk into his upper back; life returns to his eyes. He sits up and moves to the edge of the armchair. My mother sits on the bed facing him. They are so close together their knees touch. I ask my mother whether I should call the doctor. My father shakes his head. Without turning to look at me, my mother waves me away. I feel helpless, useless.

"What I should do?" I ask Petra. She has been their housekeeper and companion for twenty years. She would know best if I should send for help.

"Come, let's go. Leave them," she says.

I follow Petra out of the room, but at the doorway, I hesitate. I turn around, intending to ask my mother if she's sure my father is okay, intending to insist that I call the doctor. What I see and hear convinces me that I am wrong on two counts. They do not need the doctor, and the doubts I have harbored for years about my mother's capacity for forgiveness were badly misplaced.

"Una," my father whispers to my mother. They are huddled together, foreheads grazing each other. "One minute I was here and then I wasn't."

My mother places her hand tenderly on his. She squeezes it. "Were you afraid?"

"That's the thing, Una." He utters his characteristic guffaw, a gurgling in his throat, innocent, almost child-like surprise in his eyes. "I wasn't afraid at all. When I woke up and remembered, I wasn't afraid."

"So you see, Waldo, there's nothing to be afraid of," she coos.

I hold my breath. They are talking about death. She is eighty-nine; he is ninety-two. They know soon they will both face death. My mother has been comforted by her faith in an afterlife; my father has loved life too much to surrender to the inevitable. *Do not go gentle into that good night.* Dylan Thomas could have written these words for him.

"If this is what it means to die," my father says, "it's not bad, Una. I'm okay. I'm ready."

This is what I wanted when I married; this is why I ultimately left my husband. I wanted to die in the presence of someone I loved, someone who loved me, someone who had been kind to me, who had cared about me, who had supported me through good times and bad. Someone with whom I had history.

"Yes, Waldo," my mother responds. She keeps her eyes fixed on her husband; she soothes him; she speaks to him with great tenderness. "It won't be bad. You have been a good husband, a good father. I could not have wanted more. God knows the good man you are. He will reward you in the next life."

How I envied my parents at that moment! I needed no other proof. My mother loved her husband; she had never stopped loving him. He was comforted by her enduring love for him. If he had died that day, he would not have died alone.

My father was never afraid. Death never held him in its grip, in terror of the void. He was angry. Resentful. He wanted more time, everlasting time. But now, soothed by his wife, he remembers what he has known since he was a boy hunting in the forest, fishing in the seas. Humans too are part of the great scheme of nature, like plants, animals, and fish, to be born, to live, to die. To pass the baton to another life. "Everything in nature dies," he says to my mother. "But I'll live again in my children."

I find out later that my father had a minor stroke. It is the first of several strokes, none of which will debilitate him seriously. He will continue to clear the lawn of leaves from the mango trees; he will continue to pick up rotting oranges, limes, and sapodillas from the ground.

He will sit on the bench under the entwined mango trees and whistle to the birds. They will answer him and he will whistle back. Life will go on. All will be well. Acceptance is all.

After All These Years

21

I have been tough on my mother. Resentful. I cannot seem to forgive her for turning me out of the house before I was old enough to understand the workings of the world. For turning me out of the house is what she did. I was just sixteen. In 1960, in colonial Trinidad, a girl like me was still a child, sheltered by her middle-class family and shielded by nuns in her convent school who knew next to nothing about the evils lurking in the world except what they had read in the Bible. I had never kissed a boy; I had never gone on a date. When the sun descended and the sky darkened, I returned home from wherever I had gone. I was always chaperoned: in the day by parents, relatives, teachers, and neighbors, at night by my brothers and older cousins. But my father had landed a big position at Shell, and my parents were moving to the south. They sent me to live with my grandmother in the north, in Diego Martin. Three years later, I was on my way to Fond du Lac, Wisconsin, on a scholarship from Marian College.

What an opportunity! What a better chance you'll be getting than the chances your mother had when she was your age! That was what the neighbors said, what my relatives said.

I am eternally grateful for that scholarship from Marian College. It set me on the path to my careers as an academic and a writer, professions that have given me much satisfaction. But the singular dream that persisted from my childhood until it was shattered irrevocably late into my adulthood was to have a loving family, a husband who shared my values and hopes, happy children we raised together. I have the child, a son who more than makes up for the happiness I could have had from children I denied myself when shortly after his birth, painfully aware that my marriage was doomed, I instructed my doctor to implant an IUD in my womb which I did not remove until I entered menopause.

A better life? Nothing could make up for my despair, my utter loneliness, at the time that should have been the happiest of my life, the time before and after the birth of my son. What can compensate me for the feeling of being set adrift in a strange and hostile land with no one to rescue me, no family in America to support me? I will skip the details of the actual birth of my son. I will go straight to the night before the morning I fully expected to take him home.

It is 1976. I am in Brookdale Hospital in Brooklyn, New York. Though I have no concrete proof, I suspect my husband D— is having an affair, has been having an affair for months now. He was angry when I told him I was pregnant. We had been married just over a year. I was thirty, he was thirty-seven. He had been married before; his wife had died, leaving him with a small son. He wasn't ready to be tied down with another child and he made me feel guilty for burdening him with the added responsibility. He wanted to have fun, he said, and rumors swirled in my college that he was having fun with one of my colleagues.

I went into labor on August 10, in the middle of a

stormy night. D— drove me to the hospital and stayed by my side until I was taken on a gurney to the delivery room the next morning when my son was born, on August 11. I see D— once later that day, but he seems restless, anxious to leave. He will come and help me pack the next night, he tells me; we can take the baby home early in the morning. The next night, August 12, a nurse's aide brings me dinner; she clears my tray after I eat. I wait. I'm not worried. The nurse will bring my son to me soon so I can feed him. D— will be there for the feeding; in the morning we will take our baby home.

Half an hour later I hear footsteps, two sets; they are approaching my room. A woman enters. She is not a nurse. She is dressed in civilian clothes, a pretty bright blouse under a fashionable suit jacket. She is holding a clipboard in one hand, a pencil in the other. Behind her, in the shadows, I see a doctor. He is not my doctor. He is too young to be my doctor, and he is white. My doctor is middle-aged, and he is black.

I sit up. My heart sinks. I think the worst. "My baby! Is something wrong with my baby?"

The doctor steps forward. He is wearing a white coat; his stethoscope dangles professionally around his neck. "Mrs. H—, we know what you have done." His manner is that of judge pronouncing the verdict of the jury.

My jaw drops open. "Done?"

"No time for games, Mrs. H—. We have the proof."

The woman with the clipboard speaks up. Her tone is gentler, soothing, but her words unequivocal. "We have given the baby something, Mrs. H—. It will help him with the spitting up."

"Something?" I repeat foolishly.

"To counteract the effects of the methadone," the young doctor says sternly. He has other patients to see; he does not have time for niceties.

"Methadone?" I am in a nightmare. Soon I will wake up, I tell myself. I repeat my question. The doctor does not answer me.

The woman with the clipboard begins to write something on what I can see is some sort of official form. "Of course, you can't take your baby with you," she says. "You'll have to leave him with us. We have already reported the situation. That's why I'm here. I'm a social worker. I'm here to help you."

The room begins to spin, faster and faster. I am in a whirlwind, voices bouncing and swirling against each other. I hear the words *heroin, needles, baby spitting up, methadone*. I am a wild woman now. I strip off my gown. I do not care who sees my body, my flabby belly, my pendulous breasts. "Where? Where?" I stick out my arms; my nails scratch long ashy lines across my veins. "Where are the needle marks? Where have I injected heroin into myself?"

The well-dressed, perfectly coiffed social worker is taken aback. She pulls her clipboard to her chest, armor to protect herself from the crazy woman I have become.

"Where?" I slide my hands down my bare legs. I am trembling all over.

The woman brings the clipboard closer to her chest. It is her heart she wants to protect now, the heart I can see is bleeding for me. "It's a mistake," she whispers to the doctor. "I think we made a mistake here."

D— arrives later. I am shaking, not so much with

anger as with fear. *What have they done to my son? Why haven't they brought him to me?* I cannot speak. D— has to grab me roughly by my shoulders and shake me to get me to speak.

"They have given him methadone." I force the words through clenched muscles tightening my throat. "We have to stop them."

"Calm down, calm down," D— says.

My husband's girlfriend is waiting for him. He is impatient. This incident—that his child could have been given methadone—is an inconvenience for him. Though I do not know this now, the day we bring our son home, he will disappear for week. So he does not need my craziness, my paranoia (he seems to believe) interrupting his plans. "Calm down. Calm down," he repeats. I cannot calm down.

We go to see the director of the hospital. He has heard from the social worker and the doctor, of course. He is ready for us, ready with his lies.

—No, not at all. We haven't given your son methadone.

—But the doctor said—

—He's an intern. He misunderstood. Misspoke.

—And the woman who was with him?

—She apologized. It was a mistake. She went to the wrong room.

—Then I want to take my son home *now*. Not tomorrow. *Tonight.*

—Well, we can't do that. Hospital rules.

—What rules?

—We have to get permission from the pediatrician.

—I'm his mother. I want to take him home now.

There is silence. I wait. The director shuffles some papers on his desk.

—Mrs. H—. His voice is syrupy, patronizing. Mrs. H—, I know how you feel. I would feel the same way if I were in your situation, but I can assure you that we did not give your son methadone. As I said, the doctor misspoke. He is young, he didn't understand. We will take perfect care of your son, I promise. We have to be sure that nothing is wrong with him. The spitting up, you know . . . He shuffles the papers again. He avoids my eyes.

—All babies spit up, I say. I am glaring at him, my eyes on fire.

—Go home, Mrs. H—. Come back Monday.

It is Friday. They have already reported me as a negligent mother, an abusive mother, my son in need of government protection. The social services office is closed; the staff has gone home for the weekend. I will have to wait until Monday. They do not tell me this, but I know that this is the case.

What did I expect my mother to do when I told her what had happened to me? I was in America, the land of opportunity. Everything will work out. Everything works out in America.

My mother does not understand American racism; she does not understand that here her class does not trump her color. I have been harsh with my brother Richard, but there is some truth in what he says. I rail against his insistence that only in America does he confront racism, arguing that it is his light skin that gives him a pass in Trinidad, privilege to enter the island's high society without question. But when I say this to him, I am also aware I am only partially right. If he were pitch black and he were a doctor, the very same doors in Trinidad would be open to him.

I am a college professor. I was a college professor at the time I had my son, but my profession, my class, counted for nothing when that young, inexperienced white doctor, carrying with him years of American history, deep-rooted prejudices that define a black man or woman as less than a white man or woman, walked into my hospital room. He didn't have to ask who I was, what I did. He simply looked at me and assumed.

Fixed in my mother's mind are images of Americans she had seen in the 1950s movies she loves. She does not notice there are no black people in those movies, or if there are, they are saucer-eyed, big grins plastered on lips exaggerated to make them more servile and farcical. Those black people are not in her social class. My mother identifies with the Americans in her social class; it does not occur to her that all of them are white.

To my mother Americans are incredibly polite. Even the gas station attendant says thank you. In the department store, the saleslady follows her. I tell her the gas station attendant wants a tip; the saleslady is afraid she'll steal something. My mother doesn't believe me.

So I tell her that her son, the surgeon, cannot drive his Mercedes in New Jersey without being stopped by the police at least once a week. To avoid confrontation, he allows other cars to pass him; he drives strictly within the speed limit. "That's what he *should* do," my mother replies. "One should always obey the law." When I ask her about the other cars that were speeding, she shakes her head. "One cannot always count on luck," she declares.

What if I tell her what has happened to her son just recently, in 2011? She is no longer alive; I cannot tell her. So I'll tell you, Reader.

It's New Year's Eve, my brother's patient is in labor; it's a difficult case. The hospital calls; the woman is fighting for her life. My brother doesn't wait to change his clothes. He jumps in his Mercedes dressed as he is, in an old pair of jeans and a torn sweater, and he speeds down the turnpike. The inevitable happens: the police stop him. He shows the officer his ID. He is a doctor. "Oh yeah?" the officer sneers. It is clear he thinks the ID is a fake. "What hospital?" My brother explains the situation. It is urgent, dire. "Let me see your hospital papers." My brother has learned to hold his temper. He has learned to be cool. America's black president is cool, too cool, his critics say. He should show some real emotion, they say. How can we tell when he is really angry? Does he have real feelings? But black people in America know that emotions can get you locked up. They stay cool. They say, "Yes sir. No sir," when they speak to the police.

"Here is the phone number, sir," my brother says. "Call the hospital."

The officer grins and withdraws. He does not call the hospital. After all, it's New Year's Eve; everybody wants to party. "Okay, but let that be the last time," he warns, then winks at my brother. "Do me a favor, lay off the champagne. Okay, man?"

My brother tells us this story and we listen in silence. "I suppose it was because I was dressed so casually," he says. "The officer couldn't imagine a doctor would be dressed the way I was."

We nod in agreement. No one believes what my brother has just said and neither does he, but for a moment we allow his excuse to take the edge off the humiliation we feel. No matter how high we may climb up the professional ladder, we will always be judged as inferior. My mother did not understand that. She was a brown-skinned woman, but doors parted for her in Trinidad. She belonged to the island's upper-middle class.

Why didn't my mother come to New York when I needed her, when I found myself accused of being a heroin addict, an abusive mother? Why didn't she take my side? "It was probably as the hospital said, a mistake. Your son is doing fine now." That's what she made herself believe.

Paul McCartney was sixteen when he wrote the lyrics to his song "When I'm Sixty-Four." A young man in love worries about the future. Will his girlfriend still love him when he's sixty-four? He asks the question that troubles his spirit: *Will you still need me, will you still feed me / When I'm sixty-four?* I am sixty-four.

Does my mother love me? I do not have my answer, though my future is here now. My mother sent me away when I was still a child, then she abandoned me again. Years have passed. I have allowed my resentment to simmer quietly, to fuse into the undying embers of an ancient grievance. But I am not a child now. It is 2008. My mother is still alive. There is time for me to rid myself of this stone in my heart.

22

And a miracle happens. I am a skeptic, but what else can I call the events that lead to my coming to Trinidad three times in 2008, the year my mother dies? What stars had to be aligned? *God moves in a mysterious way, His wonders to perform.* So writes the eighteenth-century English poet William Cowper. How often had I heard my Anglican grandmother sing the hymn that was set to those words!

I am awarded a sabbatical leave, and without much forethought I decide to spend the spring semester in Trinidad. I call my friend, the eminent scholar Dr. Kenneth Ramchand. He was then associate provost at the newly established University of Trinidad and Tobago and head of the arts department. He tells me I can teach a course in creative writing if I am willing to forgo my usual salary. Once we come to an agreement, I call my parents. I will be staying with them for three months. If my mother feels any trepidation, as is usually the case when any of her foreign-based children visit (she would repaint rooms, send Petra in a tizzy to clean and polish the brass, buff the tiled floors, bake special breads), she gives me no evidence. "Come," she says. "Your father and I would welcome a long visit from you. It's about time."

It's about time. Is she thinking what I am thinking? Is

she thinking it's about time we resolve the unspoken tensions that persist between us?

I arrive in mid-February. In the lobby of the airport, returning Trinidad nationals are waving and shouting happily to families and friends who rush to greet them. Cars are waiting for them at the curb, engines throbbing. Young men—husbands, sons, uncles, nephews—fling open doors and dash out to grab suitcases. Another explosion of greetings. More hugs and kisses. The parking police officer indulges them. He grins and waits patiently. Finally, he calls out to them: "Okay, okay. Enough now. You have time for all that when you get home."

There is no one at the airport to greet me. In the past my father would have been here, but he is too old to drive now and my two sisters and my brother are at work. I must take a taxi like the rest of the tourists. I am awash by deep feelings of loss. I have come back to Trinidad, but not to home. I turn away from the happy, raucous crowd.

The cab driver senses my foreignness. "We just finish building this airport," he says, his hand sweeping across the length of the new building. "You see the Carnival costumes inside? Nice, 'eh? You know we have the best carnival in the world." His face is aglow with pride.

I am tempted to say I'm a national too, I am part of "we"; I know our history, I know about Carnival, but I can tell he has rehearsed this speech for people who look like me. Even with my brown skin, I am pale from the cold winter months away from the sun. My white linen shirt is glued to my back, drenched with perspiration.

"Number one in the world, for sure. Better than

Rio." He talks on, pacing his words, pronouncing them as carefully as he would for the tourists who have a hard time understanding the Trinidadian accent. In the end, the *th*'s prove too much of an effort for him and he gives up. "What you tink of de pictures of de prime ministers on de wall? We have one for de queen too? We was a colony of England, you know. But all dat done." When he drops me off, I give him a big tip. In American dollars.

My mother is all smiles when she sees me. She throws one arm around my neck, the other across my back, crushing my ribs. She kisses me. This time it's not the usual peck, her lips barely grazing my skin. It's a full kiss she gives me; it lingers, and I feel the warm, wet softness of her mouth on my cheek.

This is my first indication that my mother wants to break down the wall between us, that for her it's about time too. When we part, I reach for her hand; her fingers are icy cold.

My father shuffles to the gate to meet me, but there is no doubt he is delighted I am here. He can't seem to stop chuckling. His eyes twinkle mischievously. "You looking good or you good looking?" He laughs uproariously, tickled by his witticism.

Petra, too, is happy to see me. "The house get so quiet sometimes," she says. I imagine it gets quieter when she leaves in the late afternoon. My mother and father are alone when she goes. Their old gardener has retired. With the exception of Petra, all the people who now work for my parents are strangers. My sisters and brother drop by, but not daily.

Is this the price for ambition? Did my parents think of this possibility, that they could be left virtually alone in their old age if all their children go abroad?

My father follows me to the girls' room. "Let her un-pack, Waldo," my mother says querulously. "She's just arrived. Give her time." My father stands sheepishly at the door.

We have lunch. I sit next to my mother. She passes the dish of fried chicken to me. "I didn't know if you liked it stewed, so I told Petra to fry it. Like Kentucky Fried Chicken, you know." She grins shyly.

She means to say she does not know if I can still stomach Trinidadian food, the way they make stewed chicken with burnt sugar and lots of spices.

"I like fried chicken, but I love it stewed too," I respond. My mother clears her throat and exchanges knowing glances with Petra, who has been watching me too as I bite into the chicken.

After lunch, my mother goes to her room to watch the soaps. My father retires to the couch in the veranda. Soon he is asleep. My sisters tell me that lately his naps after lunch last until teatime. Old age, they say, the body preparing itself for the long sleep. I am glad I am here before it's too late.

We have tea at four with hot scones Petra baked and jam. My mother and I talk around each other, about the latest news in America, the latest news in Trinidad. She asks about my son, about my work, about my friends she has met on her trips to New York. She veers away from anything too personal. She does not ask about my life, though I know she wants to know if I am happy, if all is going well. If I have met someone who could be with me for the rest of my life. There is always hope; I could get an annulment like Jacqueline and remarry in the church.

I could have a husband. I answer her questions but I tell her also that my life is full. I have good friends, and my son and his family are a comfort to me. Her eyes brighten. I am pleased to know I have put her at ease.

My sisters and brother visit but soon leave to be with their families. Darkness comes quickly and suddenly. I am shading my eyes from the glare of the sun one moment and the next I need clear glasses to find my way to the light switch on the wall. My father retires early. At exactly at six thirty, he closes the drapes in the dining room and living room and switches off most of the indoor lights. He leaves one dim light on in the veranda. My mother complains. "It's like a tomb in here." But she follows my father to the bedroom.

I go to the den and switch on the TV. I find myself hungry for news from America. Only two American news stations are available, CNN and Fox. In New York I never watch Fox News, but now I am so anxious to hear American voices, I find myself switching back and forth from CNN to Fox. Two hours later, I am about to turn in for the night when I hear my mother's footsteps padding along the corridor. "Is everything all right?" she asks me. I nod and smile. "I love you," she says, and turns away before I can respond.

But would I have responded? Would I have said, "I love you too," as my son always says to me?

It has been two years now since my mother has begun ending all my telephone calls to her with a quick and abrupt, "I love you." She puts down the phone before I can answer. Now she has said the same words to me in person and I am strangely uncomfortable.

I make up my mind to find some sort of distraction

the next night. I call a friend who has lived many years abroad and has returned to retire in Trinidad. We cannot meet tomorrow but the following day she will have someone pick me up and bring me to a small dinner party she is hosting.

I teach the next day. By six thirty, the house is shrouded in silence and darkness again except for the insistent croaking of the frogs outside, the drone of voices on the TV in my parents' bedroom, and the light in the den where I find myself oddly entertained by the rantings of Bill O'Reilly. I can hardly wait to go to my friend's home tomorrow.

The man who picks me up the next evening tells me he cannot bring me back. My friend assures me she will, though I will have to wait until all her guests have left. It is two in the morning when she finally drives me back to my parents' home. My mother is up, waiting for me in the kitchen. "I was worried. I wanted to be sure you were safe. These are not good times in Trinidad. The crime, you know . . ." She had obviously not slept a wink. Old, her body failing, she had summoned the strength to stay awake for me. Still, I cannot get my tongue to say the words I love you, though they stir in my heart. My mother does not repeat them to me, though I am certain she wants to.

And so we continue day after day, night after night. We are stubborn, fixed in our habits. Or is it that we don't need words to express what we know each other feels? The proof is in the doing, in the behavior, I tell myself. I am here, in her house, to spend time with her.

Sometimes, when I do not have to teach, I sit with my mother in her bedroom as she follows the soaps on TV or watches the religious channel. Sometimes, instead of going to the veranda, my father stretches out on the bed, next to his wife, and naps. One afternoon, my mother's favorite soap is cut short for the simultaneous airing of the pope's visit to New York. My mother does not mind; she is anxious to see the pope. I am anxious too, but for a bit of New York, a bit of home. From the minute the program begins my mother's eyes are trained on the TV, tracking the procession that precedes the pope's entrance to the church. I am glued to the TV too, but not for the pope. I am searching the crowd pressed against the restraining ropes, hoping to see someone I know, a familiar face.

The pope arrives. Suddenly my mother, who has been sitting on the edge of the bed, rears back, her face wrinkled with disgust. She makes wide waving gestures with her arms, crossing them back and forth in front of the TV. "I don't believe in all that," she says, shaking her head vigorously.

I can barely trust my ears. "You don't believe in the pope?"

"All that gold around him, all those fancy vestments!"

I stare at her. "*Him?*"

"Yes, the pope. What does all that gold around him have to do with God, or the poor people who are dying of starvation and disease?"

My sentiments exactly! "Yes. What does all that gold have to do with God?"

"Or Jesus."

I hold my breath. My mother is criticizing the religion she has always obeyed slavishly, which she had made us, her children, obey slavishly when we lived under her roof!

"Jesus was born in a manger to a poor woman," she says, fanning the air dismissively.

I am more relieved than I am in shock. I release my breath. We are bonding, my mother and I. It is a baby step we take, to be sure, but a beginning.

Two days later, my mother's prayer group arrives. "One of the hardest things about growing old," my mother says to me, "is that by the time you are my age, all your friends have died." She has always been a social butterfly. My father was married to her and to his work, and when he could no longer do his work, all that was left for him was my mother. But my mother made new friends. She not only joined a neighborhood ladies club, she also became a member of a prayer group that is meeting in her home today.

The members arrive together in one car. I leave the veranda and go to my bedroom, but soon my mother calls out: "Elizabeth! Come! We have a question for you."

All the women in the prayer group are younger than my mother. One of them sits imperiously opposite her, her back ramrod straight. She turns to face me when I walk through the glass sliding door into the veranda, her eyes challenging mine. *Your mother may have a question for you, but I don't,* her eyes seem to say. *I'm the expert here. Don't you come with your liberal American foolishness and confuse my friends.*

"P— says . . ." My mother points to the woman with the ramrod back and repeats her interpretation of a passage in the Bible. "What do you think, Elizabeth?"

My first instinct is that she wants to show me off, Elizabeth her professor daughter, but something in her smile, sly like the proverbial Cheshire cat, tells me that this time is different. I sense a setup. She wants me on her side. The younger women have their darts pointed at her. She wants us to do battle together against them.

I sit down next to my mother. I can feel her body tensing up. *Will I play along? Or will I be her lost American daughter who is no longer on her team?* I smile at her and she relaxes. "I may not be right," I say to the group, "but this is what I think." I give my interpretation; I talk about metaphor, symbol, allegory. I pepper my response with historical, biblical, and literary references. I elaborate. I cite long quotes by heart. The women are impressed, even the imperious one backs down. My mother is pleased. "Why don't you stay for the rest of the discussion?" she suggests. I stay, proud that I have been there to help her.

We are getting along, inch by inch, day by day. I go to Sunday Mass with my parents. My mother does not have to ask me to join them. I'm dressed, ready to go, when Wally pulls up in the driveway to take us to church. I sit in the pew next to them. The church is crowded; there are people standing in the back and along the sides, but the place in the pew where my parents have sat for years is empty. The usher quietly asks strangers and newly arrived parishioners to move if by chance they have seen the empty spot and have not been forewarned. *That's Mr. and Mrs. Nunez's place.*

I have never seen my father pray, but at Mass he knows all the prayers, all the hymns. When the priest turns to the congregation for response, my father's voice is the loudest. He sings off-key, the words warbling out of his mouth. Children giggle, parents admonish them sternly and send my mother sympathetic smiles.

For my father, the high point comes when the priest asks the congregation to give each other the sign of peace. My father kisses my mother quickly on the cheek, kisses me, and he is out of the pew, up and down the aisles, shaking hands, greeting the parishioners. They know him by name. *How are you doing, Mr. Nunez? How are your children?* My mother, ever elegant, remains standing in her place, acknowledging their good wishes with a gracious smile.

It takes my parents almost an hour to get into the car after Mass. I watch as people crowd around them, introducing relatives, visitors, children. Wally is patient. "This is the day they wait for all week," he tells me. "At least Dad does. Mum goes out, but Dad sticks to the house all week. He won't go anywhere, except to take long walks in the afternoon."

Later, as he does every Sunday, Wally drives my parents to the home of one my sisters, either to Jacqueline's home or Karen's. My sisters prepare an elaborate lunch. They put out their best dishes, their best silverware, their best stemmed glasses for my parents. The food they serve is beautifully prepared, color coordinated, and delicious. This Sunday, lunch is at Jacqueline's. My sisters and brother talk and laugh with each other, they exchange memories. When Jacqueline speaks of the distant past, I am animated; I find a space to break into their reveries. "Do you remember the times we spent in Toco?"

Every vacation—Christmas, Easter, the August holidays—my parents took us to the countryside to spend a week or more at the rest houses in Cedros, Mayaro, Blanchisseuse, Toco. The English had built these vacation cottages on the coastal villages in Trinidad, not for us of course, but for their expatriate employees, though my father could not be denied one of the perks that had been given to the Englishman he succeeded. The English, after all, took pride in their sense of fairness, especially when it was not inconvenient for them, and I had spent some of the happiest days of my youth at the rest house in Toco.

Karen cuts me short in the middle of my reminiscences. She remembers the great times they had on the other islands, in Tobago, St. Vincent, Grenada, Barbados. What fun they had staying at the hotels on the beach!

Hotels? I had known only rustic rest houses in the countryside in Trinidad. But I had long ago left the island; I was in America; I had missed those days.

"Your father believed in keeping the family together," my mother says.

How well I know the truth of what she says. In the box where I store my most treasured possessions there is a letter from my father. The stationery is elegant, most likely chosen by my mother. It is lime green in color, the insides of the envelope a darker green. A vine of flowers in shades of green runs along the sides of heavy expensive paper. My father thanks me in the letter for making the trip from New York to Trinidad to celebrate his fiftieth wedding anniversary. In his sweeping, handsome handwriting, stemmed letters flowing confidently below each line, he writes:

Dear Elizabeth,
Thank you for joining with your brothers and sisters to celebrate with us our Golden Anniversary.

We trust you will always remain together as a closeknit family caring for each other.

May God bless you.
Mom & Dad

Just as I am sure, given my mother's exquisite taste, that she was the one who selected the stationery, I am sure too that it was she, forever hopeful, forever praying we would all return to the Catholicism of our childhood, who had my father add the words, *May God bless you.* She signs *Mom*; I recognize her handwriting. My father signs *& Dad.* Though my brothers and their wives have taken to calling them Mom and Dad, my sisters and I continue to address them as Mummy and Daddy, and with American television beaming daily into their bedroom, my parents too eventually began signing their holidays cards to us using the American shorthand. My siblings tell me that each of them, all eleven of us, received a similar handwritten letter. The letters are dated May 1, 1993, one week after our parents' anniversary.

Karen is sitting close to my mother. She will not allow my father to take all the praise for keeping the family together. She has told me more than once that our mother considered her her best friend. Now she interjects: "You too, Mummy. You kept the family together."

"Yes, me too," my mother concedes.

My father nods in agreement and then slips away to an armchair near a window. Soon he is fast asleep.

Talk turns to a past that is familiar to my sisters and brother, a past light-years ago when I was in my twenties, thirties, and forties, living in America. I have nothing to say; no memories to add. When I leave my sister's home I am sad, slightly depressed. How comfortable they are with each other! What history they share! They speak of people I do not know, have never met, of events I know nothing about. Their jokes fly over my head. I laugh with them, but I do not understand much of the humor in the stories they tell. Sometimes I am forced to ask them to slow down, my ears no longer tuned to the accents of my homeland. I want to make history; I want to connect the line from my childhood to my present, from Toco to this moment, but my history has been broken by my years in America.

Early the next morning, before the sun has had a chance to rise above the horizon, I am awakened by the clanging of dishes in the kitchen. I hear voices, female voices. I tiptoe to the kitchen. My mother is there, fully dressed in slacks and a loose silk shirt. Petra is next to her. They are huddled together packing sandwiches in a tin box. She is going on a picnic with her prayer group, my mother says. I run to my room and bring out my oversized designer handbag. "Here." I give her my brand-new Louis Vuitton bag. "Put the box in there," I say.

She is pleased. "I'll look real stylish today." And she does when she holds the bag against her tan slacks.

I ask her where the prayer group will be having the picnic.

"At a retreat house on Salybia Bay," she answers.

I gasp. Salybia Bay is on the north coast. It is dark now; it will still be dark when she and her group reach the north coast and begin the dangerous trip to Salybia Bay through winding, narrow roads that plunge down steep precipices to a windswept sea hurling against gigantic black rocks scattered along the shoreline. My mother is eighty-nine, only a couple of months away from ninety. She may think of herself as young as the women in her prayer group, but she is not as agile.

"What if something happens to the car along the way?" I ask.

My mother, who I know to be afraid of rough seas, afraid of the dark, brushes me away. "You have such a vivid imagination, Elizabeth."

And I remember that in 1949, afraid of the sea, afraid of the dark, she went on a ship by herself across the Atlantic Ocean, no land in sight for days, because she missed her husband.

23

There is so much I do not know about my mother. At Sunday lunch at Jacqueline's, I had remained silent when Karen defended my mother and refused to allow my father full credit for keeping the family together. And the truth is that when I recalled the letter my parents had sent me, thanking me for celebrating their fiftieth wedding anniversary with them, it was my father I credited, not my mother, as if it were not my mother's idea too, as if she were not involved in its composition.

The images I have cemented in my mind now seem all wrong, twisted. My mother is not as fragile as I thought, nor is she a social snob or a self-righteous religious fanatic. She is as caring of my father as he is of her. I see that now. Things that irritated me before begin to make sense seen through her eyes. I begin to notice how much she worries that my father is spending too much time alone, too much time in the house, too much time dozing off.

Every day my mother now drags me into a conspiracy with her to get my father out of the house. She sends me to the supermarket with a list of groceries she insists she needs. "Take your father with you," she says.

Inside the supermarket my father stops to talk to the young men and women who stack the shelves and serve

prepared food from behind the deli counter. They indulge him, as do the burly men who lug heavy cases of
groceries from their trucks to the store. The manager
seems to know my father, or acts as if he does, and customers in line wait patiently as he chats up the female
cashiers. Suffering from dementia, my father has never
lost his eye for a beautiful woman.

The next day my mother sends me out with my father
again. "Why couldn't you have put this on the list yesterday?" I complain. My mother smiles at me coyly. The
same thing happens all over again the next day and the
next. My mother sends me out to buy two onions and
a head of garlic, and then a pound of onions and two
sticks of butter the following day. I get her a pound of
potatoes on Wednesday, and another pound on Thurs-
day. My father goes with me each time, chats with the
customers and the workers, and flirts with the pretty
young women, who giggle delightedly. It takes me a
week but eventually I catch on; I figure out my mother's
strategy. She has divided her grocery list into the days of
the week so that every day my father has an adventure,
every day I have an occasion to take him somewhere.

My mother's methods are not mine. I am wary of
secrets, of subterfuge. I tend to be direct. Why not say
what you mean? But my mother's tactics work. In the
supermarket, chatting with the workers and customers,
flirting with the women, my father's spirits are raised.
He is in a good mood when we return home. "I'm going
to check on my neighbor down the road," he says. And
off he goes. He is no longer the old man nodding off to
sleep on the couch.

One day I tell my mother that she has been lucky to

have such a long and good marriage. The minute I say
this, I realize I have opened myself to tripping into a
quagmire. She has not approved of my siblings' divorces,
nor of mine. Marriage remains a sacrament for her, a
vow never to be broken. But this time my mother sur-
prises me. "D— was a nice man," she says, "but he was
not right for you."

I spend more time with my mother now. I begin to observe her habits more closely. A week ago I fumed silently to myself at her selfishness for keeping the TV on,
tuned to her religious programs, while my father shifted
restlessly on the bed. Now I wonder if I have not judged
her prematurely, if I have not allowed years of built-up
resentment to blind me. My father has lost most of his
hearing; even if she turns up the volume, he would not
be able to hear the sound. Then I notice, as if for the
first time, that she sits close to the TV, so close that if
she were to stretch out her hand, it would brush against
the screen. I remember she used to wear glasses and for
many years she needed a magnifying glass to read her
prayers. Now she looks at the TV without her glasses.
She does not open her prayer book.

She is going blind! The realization hits me full force
one evening. That is what is happening to her! She cannot see, she cannot read her prayer book; she has to listen to the prayers on the TV. I call my sister Jacqueline.
"Cataracts," she says. "Mummy is afraid to have them
removed. She's afraid she would lose what little sight
she has left." Jacqueline tells me that no one has been
able to persuade my mother to go to the ophthalmologist, neither she, nor Karen, nor Wally.

She hasn't been wearing her glasses, my mother explains when I ask, because they are broken. "Then we can get you another pair," I reply. "Okay," she says, handing me her broken glasses. "But you go. I don't need to go." She shifts her eyes to the floor. As gently as I can I say, "I think you'll need to have your eyes tested, Mummy. These are an old pair; you'll need a new prescription."

We arrange to have my mother's eyes tested by one of Judith's friends who is an ophthalmologist. We tell him of my mother's fears so when I take her to his office the path has already been cleared. Before we go in the examining room, the receptionist shows us a variety of frames. I still have not fully processed the extent to which my mother's sight has been diminished so I am swept into her game of choosing frames as if all that is needed is to replace her broken ones and get a stronger prescription for her lenses. "How much does this pair cost?" my mother asks me, taking the frames the receptionist hands her. Only later do I realize why she waits for my answer before choosing a frame.

The ophthalmologist, however, is blunt: "I can give you a prescription for a new pair of glasses, Mrs. Nunez, but you'll be wasting your money. You won't be able to see any better than you do now. You need to have surgery on your eyes."

My mother does not concede that a new prescription will be useless, but she selects the cheapest of the frames the receptionist shows us, the ones she remembers from the price tags I read for her. Even as she tries to fool me, my mother will not spend money foolishly. Memories of the days when she lived in fear that my father's salary would not be enough to feed us are hardwired in her brain.

Little by little I manage to persuade her to have the surgery. I tell her about friends who have had their cataracts successfully removed; I tell her about the new painless techniques that have been invented. She agrees to the surgery, but only on one eye, and allows me to take her to the hospital for the pre-op tests. By the time I leave for New York, my sisters have scheduled the appointment for the surgery. "You'll see, Mummy," I tell her. "You'll be able to read your prayer book as good as ever."

My sisters say I have managed a miracle. "She must really trust you," Jacqueline remarks. "We tried lots of times, but nothing we said convinced her to have the surgery." I beam.

My mother and I laugh too. I discover she has a sense of humor; she is not as rigid as I have allowed myself to believe. I take her to the Funeral Mass for one of the last of their remaining friends. It is the afternoon she came running to me, frantic with fear from a dream portending her death, or so I believed, and made me wake up my father from his afternoon slumber. It is the afternoon she gave my father a tuxedo to wear.

"We must leave now," my mother commands me. I must drive my parents to the Funeral Mass. I have taken only small trips with my father, to the grocery and back, but I reason that the church is only a few neighborhoods away and I put aside my trepidation about the Trinidad roads and take them there.

My mother directs me through the roads to the church and we arrive safely. I am confident I will be able to find my way back, but I get lost driving them home after the Funeral Mass ends. "Turn this way," my mother says, as I mistake one street for another; so few of them have signs. "No, turn that way," my father counters. I twist the steering wheel from right to left and back again as they direct and redirect me. Soon I am trundling down narrow, bumpy back roads, barely skating past open ravines. My parents continue to direct me. "No, not this way!" my mother shouts. "Yes, this way," my father insists. "You've forgotten the roads from the church to home," my mother chastises him. "Listen to me, Waldo!" "And you can't see the street signs," my father says. I brace myself for a rough ride. Back and forth they go. I recognize houses and shops I have passed minutes before. We are going in circles. They have not stopped their arguments: who has the better memory, who has the better sight. Then, mercifully, the road broadens. I am surrounded by open space, no houses in sight, patches of coarsely shorn grass, most likely cut by a farmer's scythe. My parents, who are installed in the backseat, sit forward. "Do you know where we are?" I hear my mother whisper to my father. "In some sort of forest, I think," my father whispers back. I see a sign: *University of the West Indies.* My father reads it for my mother. She doubles over with laughter. She is almost choking on her words when she says to my father, "Elizabeth wants me to go to university. I think it's a little too late for me, don't you think so, Waldo?"

Someone directs us to the highway. I am nervous but I am not willing to chance the back roads again. On one side of the road, as we approach their house, my mother spots the gigantic red letters on the marquee outside the KFC. "Pull in there, Elizabeth," she says. "I feel like having some fried chicken."

No plates, no napkins, no silverware, my mother sits

at the table in the breakfast nook and devours the fried chicken, grease running down her arm. Amazed, but delighted, I join her. My father does not say a word. He goes to the cupboard and takes out a plate, a knife, and a fork. We laugh as he maneuvers the utensils through the slippery sinews of a chicken leg, a gentleman dressed appropriately, but comically too, in a black tuxedo.

The following week, my mother invites me to join her at a concert in Queen's Hall. Her women friends are going—not her prayer group; these are the members of her upper-class ladies' club. The seats in the concert hall are not assigned. My mother and I arrive first and sit in the orchestra. Her friends arrive later and get balcony seats. The concert begins and I marvel at the talent on the stage. The steel pan orchestras are amazing; some of the players are children as young as eight years old. They play with precision and discipline, eyes glued to the conductor. Their repertoire covers classical music—Beethoven, Mozart, Tchaikovsky—and transitions to compositions by local composers. They play popular pieces too, some of the calypsos that made the road march at Carnival. I shout, "Bravo!" I clap, I yell. My mother looks around her tentatively. She casts her eyes up to the balcony. Have her fancy friends witnessed my display? I stand up. I continue to shout and yell. "Bravo!" My mother takes one last look around her and up at the balcony and decides to throw caution to the wind. She stands up too and cheers. "Bravo!" she shouts out.

We take trips with my father too. My friend Anne-Marie Stewart, who is in Trinidad, staying with her friend Maria Habib, invites my parents and me to Mount St. Benedict for afternoon tea. Once again I have occasion to witness the intimacy between my parents, how they live in the shadow of each other, trusting each other, looking out for each other, protecting each other. My father does not want to go, of course. He wants to sit in the shade of the entwined mango trees and sleep away the afternoon. My mother will not let him. "You need to exercise your mind, Waldo. You'll like talking to Elizabeth's friends."

Mount St. Benedict is the name of a Benedictine monastery. It sits high on the northern range in Trinidad. The monks used to run a boarding school for rich boys there, and now they counsel drug addicts and people afflicted with AIDS. They are famous for the honey they collect from the bees they raise and also for their special cakes and teas. They built a dining room for the public on their grounds where one can still have high tea, a tradition that endures in Trinidad though the British colonizers have been gone for over fifty years. This is where we are headed.

The road up to the mount is torturous, twisting around tight bends that plunge down sharply at the sides. I hold my breath each time Anne-Marie puts the car into another gear and it grinds around another bend. My heart does somersaults and my chest aches from the pressure of my inflated lungs. I am certain that at the next turn we will go tumbling down into bushes below us. I say this and Anne-Marie laughs at me. "Close your eyes then." I do as she says.

My parents, though, seem quite at ease. My mother engages my father in chatter with Anne-Marie and Maria. "We used to come here a lot," my mother says. "Not so, Waldo?"

My father begins reminiscing about the times he and my mother had afternoon tea at St. Benedict's, but soon he loses his way and is telling a story about his hunting days.

My mother brings him back to the present. "Do you remember the last time you drove me here, Waldo?"

"It was like yesterday," he responds, and adds ruefully, "I don't know why the children thought I should turn in my car keys."

I open my eyes and plead with my mother to defend us. "Tell him, Mummy."

"You were ninety, Waldo." My mother pokes him playfully in the ribs. "It was time."

Anne-Marie is shocked. She has laughed at my fear of the winding roads, the precipices plunging steeply down their sides, but I can tell she is aware of the danger too. She is sitting up erect, her back forward, her neck strained, her fingers wound tightly around the steering wheel. "Ninety and still driving, Mr. Nunez?" She keeps her eyes on the road.

"Would have been driving longer than that," my father says. "But the children . . ."

"But you don't mean driving here, Mr. Nunez?"

"Oh, he drove me here all right," my mother says cheerfully.

Anne-Marie is aghast. She tightens her fingers around the steering wheel as she shifts into another gear. The mountain is a solid wall on one side of the impossibly narrow road; on the other side the edge of the road drops abruptly down to the valley below.

"Yep," my father says. "Drove right up to the top. Remember, Una?" He is grinning from ear to ear.

I am so frightened I am clutching the edge of my seat.

I never would have been able to drive on this road. How did my father manage it? And at ninety! How my mother must have trusted him, placed her faith in his skills and his concern for her safety.

We have tea and cakes outside, on an open patio on the flat top of a cliff. As soon as he has his tea, my father excuses himself and walks to the edge of the land. Below, the roots of dense tall vegetation cling precariously to the soil. Birds flutter in and out of the branches. My father walks up and down along the perimeter, his hands locked behind his back, a beatific smile on his lips. My mother is terrified. "Waldo!" she shouts. "Don't be foolish. Come back here." He ignores her. She sends me to bring him back.

I walk to my father and stand next to him. I am awestruck by the beauty around us, the sky a bright blue and under it a cascade of dazzling greenery punctured here and there by dots of color—ripening fruit and a variety of flowers, red, orange, yellow, purple. In a dirt clearing at the bottom of the cliff, boys from the village are playing cricket. They are not in cricket whites. Colorful shirts, the fronts unbuttoned, flap behind their backs. Some wear vests; most are torn or powdered with dirt. Their pants, some long, some short, are frayed, no doubt hand-me-downs. I see a fast bowler; he knocks down the wicket. The boys on his side raise their arms and shout. Their voices do not reach us, but my father cheers. He cups his hands around his mouth and stands on tiptoe. "Well done!" he yells.

My mother gives up. She does not call out to my father again, but from time to time she glances his way, her brow furrowed with worry.

* * *

In my last week before I return to New York, I give a lecture for the University of Trinidad and Tobago in the magnificent building in the center of Port of Spain that houses NALIS, the National Library and Information System Authority. Dr. Ramchand has invited Trinidad's intellectual elite to hear me. My students at the university will be there too. I arrange for my parents to come. When they arrive, they are directed to the front row of the auditorium, to chairs reserved for them. My mother is bursting with pride: *Her* daughter, the child who came from *her* womb! A Nunez, but her child too. She sits with her head held high and acknowledges the people who wave to her with a self-effacing shrug of her shoulders.

My father has the same expression of astonishment on his face that he always has whenever he sees me in an academic setting. I can almost trace the rumblings in his head as he tries to reconcile the image of the child for whom he had the least expectations, the one he never taught to drive, with this woman about to command an audience. I have a photograph of him on the day I graduated with a PhD from New York University. He is sitting apart from the group that is congratulating me. His legs are crossed, his arms are folded, his head juts forward on his neck. He is staring at me, his eyes bolted wide open, a lopsided grin on his lips. He looks at me the same way now as the audience gathers in the auditorium, but soon he is distracted by my students who crowd around him. He and my mother have met them before, at another event at the university. They exchange pleasantries. It does not take long before my father's eyes are twinkling with mischievousness as he parries witticisms back and forth with them.

These are not my usual students, the ones I teach at Medgar Evers College in Brooklyn. The age range is the same, but not the levels of education nor the skin color. Most of my students at the University of Trinidad and Tobago are already professionals: a lawyer, an architect, an engineer, a photographer, a visual artist, a poet, a journalist, a businessman, the headmistress of a secondary school, the owner of a liquor store. A few are university students, but they are in their senior year or graduate school. All have elected to take my workshop in creative writing because they want to work on a novel. Like the amazing diversity of skin color and hair texture in Trinidad, my students are dark-skinned, cocoa-pod brown, chocolate brown, café au lait, pale cantaloupe, sun-kissed pink. They are African, Indian, Chinese, Syrian, Lebanese, Portuguese, French Creole, English, or a mélange of some or all of those bloods.

I think again of my response to my brother Richard. Perhaps I had been too quick to dismiss him. In all my years in America I have never taught a class with such a range of skin color, nor have I been part of an audience so casually diverse like this one I am about to address. In America there are assumptions about skin color. The incident at the hospital where my son was born would not be the only one I would experience when the color of my skin counted more than the content of my character or my years of university education. How often have I been taken for an usher at the opera, at a concert hall or theater, asked for a program or directions to a seat. The location of the restrooms! Once I was at the Met Opera

House waiting for F— outside the restroom near one of the expensive grand boxes where we were seated, and an old white man handed me his hat.

America prides itself on being a multicultural country, but people live in silos, in distinct neighborhoods one can easily identify by color and ethnicity. Here the Jews live, there the Italians, on the other side the Irish, away from them the WASPS, farther away the African Americans, and on the outskirts the West Indians, the Chinese, the Indians, and so on and so on. To achieve the kind of diversity taken so much for granted by my students at UTT, the government in America has to mandate it, but even then there are protests curiously claiming the unfairness of racial preferences.

I took my students at Medgar Evers College to see Chekhov's *Three Sisters*. At the end of the play, a group of them accompanied a pregnant classmate who needed to use the bathroom. They were turned away. "The bathrooms are not for the public," the usher told them. So perhaps Richard is telling the truth: he is not aware that he is black until he comes to America.

Malcolm Gladwell speaks of the privilege of skin tone in Jamaica and, by inference, all the Caribbean islands, but I wonder if he has not enjoyed privileges in Canada where he grew up, and later in America where he lived in the northern cities, because his father is a white man. Did Gladwell have greater access to privilege than his darker-skinned peers because his father, an Englishman and a math professor, could open doors for him that were closed to the majority of dark-skinned fathers?

But I digress.

And yet . . .

In 1968 my ex and his first wife, both African Americans, were looking for a house in Long Island. They wanted to be near the beach. The realtor took them to Long Beach Road on the edge of Hempstead where white flight had already reached panic proportions. "Yes, of course," the realtor said, "Long Beach Road leads to the beach, to Long Beach." What he did not say was that they would have to drive forty minutes to reach the beach. That same year, in 1968, my colleague whose father was an immigrant from Eastern Europe was also looking for a house in Long Island. He too wanted to be near the beach. His realtor took him to Merrick, not to a beach (he did not have money for a beach house), but to a house in front of a canal that opened up to the Great South Oyster Bay. Both men paid around $34,000 for their houses. Twenty-five years later, my ex sold his house for $138,000. My friend's father had his house on the market for $875,000. He sold it for much more. He was a recent arrival to America. He spoke English with a heavy Eastern European accent, yet he was able to reap for his progeny a huge economic advantage over my ex who traced his family roots in America back more than two hundred years.

My friend's father and people like him, even arrivals from that great European migration at the turn of the twentieth century, claim innocence. Neither they nor their ancestors were here during the brutal days of slavery, they say. Recent immigrants from Eastern Europe also fail to acknowledge that it was the civil rights movement of the '60s that forced the hand of legislators to widen the scope of America's immigration policies.

Yet white Americans continue to profit from the lingering legacy of slavery and Jim Crow laws. The color of their skin gives them a passport to access America's largesse, access that people of color rarely have.

I return to Gladwell's *Outliers*.

About the story of the success of Steve Jobs and outliers like him, Gladwell concludes:

> *We pretend that success is exclusively a matter of individual merit. But there's nothing in any of the histories we've looked at so far to suggest things are that simple. These are stories, instead, about people who were given a special opportunity to work really hard and seized it, and who happened to come of age at a time when that extraordinary effort was rewarded by the rest of society.*

A special opportunity. But what if Steve Jobs had been black? Would his family have been allowed to live in Palo Alto, in the midst of Silicon Valley? Jobs was going to a troubled school and his family wanted to move him to a school district that was safer and better. Would a realtor have taken the parents of black Steve Jobs, as they did the parents of white Steve Jobs, to a house in such an area? My ex had no such choice; he paid Long Island's outrageously high residential taxes, but we would have to pay more for his son and ours to go to private school if we wanted an education for them in a school that was safer and better than the public schools in our district. And would Bill Hewlett of Hewlett-Packard personally give the teenage black Steve Jobs spare parts just because he asked for them? Would he have given him a summer job? Would black Jobs have had the *ac-*

cess that ultimately paved the way for the success white Jobs achieved with Apple? If black Steve Jobs, like white Steve Jobs, had joined the wrong crowd in a troubled school, smoked marijuana, and allegedly done other drugs as well, he would have gone to jail.

I have digressed too far.

After the lecture, my students wait with me for the car my sisters have reserved to bring my parents home. When the car arrives, the driver jumps out and opens the back door for my parents. One of my students, already feeling warm toward my father who has been playfully teasing him, reaches for my mother's elbow. "I'll take it from here, Mr. Nunez," he says. "I'll help Mrs. Nunez in the car."

"Careful," my father warns, "that is my wife."

My young student misinterprets the seriousness in my father's voice. After all, they were joking with each other minutes ago. "That's okay, Mr. Nunez, you can trust me with your wife. I'll get her in the car safely."

"No!" my father snaps. There is no mistaking the command now. My student backs away. "I help my wife, nobody else does."

24

I come back to Trinidad two more times. In May, not long after I have returned to New York, I take a stopover flight to Trinidad on my way to Grenada. I have been invited to a conference organized by the Association of Caribbean Women Writers and Scholars, which is based in the States. Three scholars will be presenting papers on my novel *Prospero's Daughter*: Dr. Sandra Pouchet from the University of Miami; Dr. Hyacinth Simpson from Ryerson University in Toronto; and Dr. Jennifer Sparrow, a colleague from Medgar Evers College. Jennifer and I decide to take her daughter and my granddaughter with us to the conference. The girls are around the same age. Sophie, Jennifer's daughter, is seven and Jordan, my granddaughter, is eight. My parents have never met Jordan, and my mother, much more than my father, is eager to see her.

Our stay in Trinidad is too brief on the way out to Grenada, but on the return flight to New York, the stopover is five hours long. We take a cab to my parents' home. I have called my mother and she and my father meet us at the front gate. I introduce Jordan to my mother. "This is your great-granny, Jordan," I say. I've already alerted her that grandmothers in Trinidad are called Granny, not Grandma. Still, Jordan is an independent American girl and I cannot be certain what will come out of her mouth. She giggled when I told her to address her great-grandmother as Great-Granny. To Jordan, grannies are the stuff of dark children's stories. The wolf in *Red Riding Hood* was dressed like Granny. But Jordan steps forward and an extraordinary thing happens. My granddaughter, who is usually reticent, especially with people she does not know, wraps her arms around my mother's waist and presses her head against her chest, and my mother, usually reserved, pulls Jordan to her in a tight embrace. Jennifer wipes away a tear and the muscles in my throat constrict. My mother is hugging the granddaughter of her daughter as if the years have rolled back and she is finally able to do what she has always wished she had done decades ago. Her arms are around Jordan, but it is me, her first child, her daughter, she draws to her heart.

Petra brings us tea, and afterward my mother shows us her garden. *June too soon*, says the children's song about the coming of the hurricanes that blast the Caribbean almost every year. Trinidad is lucky; it is situated in the doldrums, between latitudes just below the hurricane belt. It gets hit with rainstorms, but not hurricanes. This year, however, neither May nor June is too soon for the rainstorms. The rain poured down in late May, the week before we arrive, and soaked the dry-season earth so my mother's garden is resplendent with bright colors and new green foliage.

The girls are not interested in the garden. To my surprise, I see they are chatting happily with my father. I cannot imagine what he could be saying to them to hold their attention. More and more, especially in the last few months, my father's words have been drifting in and out of each other, rarely making sense. I wonder too, even if he has a moment of clarity, whether he would understand their strong Yankee accent, peppered as it is with the latest popular expressions I can barely decode myself, but my father seems to be responding to the girls and they to him, so I turn away and join my mother who wants to show us her prized orchids which have outdone themselves this year.

Jennifer is in awe of the purple and white sprays that glitter in the sun. I am bowled over by the ginger lilies. My mother grows them in enormous clumps not far from the entwined mango trees. Out of a dense cluster of long dark green leaves come the long sprays of ginger lilies, some in groups of white, some pink, some dark red. These are not lilies in the usual sense one thinks of them in temperate climates, a single flower blooming at the tip of a long, thin stem. These are tropical lilies, the petals beginning almost halfway up thick stems and rising layer by layer to the top. I want to take them back with me to New York.

"You could hide them in your suitcase," my mother suggests with a wicked twinkle in her eyes. She knows about 9/11. She knows no one who looks like me is likely to escape the notice of the customs officers.

My father is in the midst of a tall tale as we walk toward him. We can see him gesticulating wildly, his arms flinging in the air. At times he stomps his feet and does a little dance. The girls are listening attentively. They do not notice when we reach them. My father sees me and stops his story. The girls groan in unison. They are not ready to leave when we tell them it's time to go. "One more story, Grandpa," Jordan pleads.

I return to Trinidad in July, this time for three days. I am helping Joy Bramble, the owner of the *Baltimore Times*, organize a Caribbean writers conference in Antigua. Joy is originally from Montserrat, but her family was forced to migrate to Antigua when the 1997 volcano on the Soufrière Hills blew up, burying almost the entire island under rivers of fiery lava. Joy lives in America now, but feels indebted to Antigua which had welcomed her family. This conference, her second, is her way of repaying the island for its generosity. She plans to donate much of the proceeds from the conference to help rebuild the library in Antigua, most of which had been demolished by a fire years earlier. Joy hopes to interest the University of Trinidad and Tobago in collaborating with her and so expand the scope and audience of the conference. We arrive on a Friday night, and will leave on Sunday in the late afternoon. I need to meet with Joy and Dr. Ramchand on Saturday night, so my only free time will be during the day.

Sunday will be my mother's ninetieth birthday. We have no intimations of the possibility, but my mother will die approximately one month from that day.

My father, who has lost the habit of checking off the days on his calendar, has not forgotten that his wife's birthday is in July. As soon as I arrive, he consults with me. "What date in July?" he asks. I tell him her birthday will be on Sunday. "Then you must take me to the store on Saturday to get a present for her and a card," he says.

What can my father buy his wife that she does not already have? "Some kind of jewelry," he tells me. "She loves jewelry." Then he hesitates. "Or perfume. She always smells nice."

On Saturday morning, I take my father to the jewelry

store. The owner knows him and makes a swift dash toward us. My father has made many purchases for my mother in this store; the jeweler knows what she has and does not have. He suggests a gold medal for her gold chain. "Something religious," he explains. "You know Mrs. Nunez is a religious woman." He shows my father a medal depicting Mary, the mother of God. I am certain my mother has many medals with the imprint of a drawing of Mary, but I hold my tongue. It does not matter what my father buys her; it matters only that he gets a present for her. My father takes the medal, but just before he pays for it, he changes his mind. He'll get her a brooch. He points to a gold rose perched on the end of a pin.

We walk over to the card store. My father goes directly to the birthday section, to the area tagged with the sign *For my wife*. I stand behind him and wait patiently as he reads one card and then another. The salesgirl, pretty and very young, snickers. I glare at her. My father moves slowly, step by step along the row of cards, picking up one, returning it to the rack, and picking another. He comes to the end, shakes his head, and returns to the beginning of the row. I have no appointments; I can wait for him all morning. "Take your time, Daddy," I say, shooting another stern look at the salesgirl who scurries to the back of the display counter. Finally, my father picks a card. "Una will like this one." It's a card that expresses a husband's undying love for his wife. *For all eternity*, the card says.

Our dinner meeting with Dr. Ramchand does not yield much, a delicious meal but little more. Dr. Ramchand has invited the provost to join us, but I sense that changes are afoot at the university and neither Dr.

Ramchand nor the provost is on secure ground with the positions they currently hold. In any case, I console myself, Joy has had a chance to catch up with old friends in Trinidad and I have been able to be with my parents for the third time this year, and on my mother's birthday.

My father has already given my mother the card and the present when I enter their bedroom early in the morning before breakfast to wish my mother happy birthday. She is beaming, holding the card in her hand. "Look, Elizabeth. Look what your father gave me." I see the jewel box open on her night table, the brooch still inside. She follows my eyes. "It's pretty," she says, "but look at the card!" She shows it to me, but she does not give it to me. She opens it and reads the words aloud. "*For all eternity*. This old man knows how to romance an old woman."

"A beautiful lady," my father rejoins.

My two sisters and my brother come to the house after lunch. One of my sisters-in-law, Marjorie, comes too. She is married to my youngest brother, Roger, who has his medical practice in Mississippi. Marjorie is a senior partner at a major law firm in Trinidad. Their marriage has already lasted a quarter century. I do not know how they manage this long-distance relationship separated by an ocean and miles of land. I have many times thought they should seek other partners, but my mother has been steadily behind them, supporting them. *What God has joined together* . . . I cannot quarrel with her reasoning as it applies to Marjorie and Roger. Together, Marjorie and my brother have raised a beautiful, brilliant, and well-adjusted daughter, Regan, who is in her last year of law school at the University of Michigan.

Marjorie has brought a cake and candles. Petra has made a special fruit drink and tiny fruit pies. She stands in the back, a respectful distance from where we have gathered. I call out to her: "Come, join us, Petra." My mother frowns at me. I do not know whether she is jealous of the attention I am paying to Petra or whether she disapproves of having her helper join us as if she were one of us, an equal. I still bristle at these last vestiges of the strictures of a class system we inherited from the British, which persist in spite of our political independence. It's my mother's birthday, so I don't insist when Petra says, "I fine where I stay." I notice none of my sisters encourage her to come closer.

After we have blown out the candles and have sung happy birthday, one of my sisters, the one who admittedly is my mother's favorite, launches into a spirited retelling of an incident that occurred on her job in which she came out victorious. My mother, who usually gives this sister her full attention, seems distracted. She does not make the appropriate sounds of approval at the points in the tale where my sister expects applause, perhaps not literally, but the usual enthusiastic encouragement. My mother's smiles seem forced and her eyes are dull.

The taxi comes for me while the party is still going on. I say my goodbyes to my siblings. I hug my father, kiss my mother. She trails me to the gate. I am about to go through it when she pulls me back. The hug she gives me, her arm locked around my neck, almost strangles me. "I love you," she whispers. And I respond, "I love you too, Mummy." It is the last time I will see her alive.

25

My mother is to be buried tomorrow. I must finish the eulogy and give it to Jacqueline so it can be printed in time for the Mass in the morning. My siblings have gone their separate ways. To give me space to think and write, they say. I leave the breakfast room and go to the dining room. There I am surrounded by my mother's treasured collections. Against one wall is a glass cabinet stocked with delicate china, dinner sets and tea sets she used only on special occasions. Against the opposite wall is a credenza. If I open the drawers I will find my mother's prized silverware.

What was the point of having all these only to use them rarely? Why keep them shut up like an exhibit in a museum?

My American friend Lynne LaSala has an expensive china set. I admired it and bought some pieces for myself. I put them in my cabinet and closed the door. I was visiting Lynne one day for lunch and she served me with her expensive china. I expressed surprise.

"I use this set every day," she said.

"Even when you are alone?"

"I bought it because I liked it a lot. It makes me happy to eat from it."

Today. *Now*. That's what counts. Not yesterday or tomorrow. My mother kept her china set shut up in a cabinet. If she could speak now, would she say she had been foolish to deny herself the pleasure of touching and using these things she loved?

Would she say the same about me, her daughter? She loved me, yet it took years for those three little words to leave her tongue. *I love you.* Like her special china, they were words to be used on special occasions, not for everyday use.

And what about my part? I had drawn an iron gate across my heart. I was the good daughter, the dutiful daughter, making sure to call my mother once a week, to visit her in Trinidad at least once a year, to buy her clothes, shoes, to do whatever she asked me to, without complaint, no matter how ridiculous. Once it got into my mother's head that she wanted a cookware set she had seen on cable TV. The promoter promised miracles. The cookware would make food tastier, juicier. My mother desperately wanted it. Each time we spoke on the phone she would sing the praises of the cookware. I didn't tell her that the promoter was just doing his job, that he had probably never used the cookware himself. I didn't say there were fourteen parts to the cookware and it would be costly and cumbersome for me to bring it for her in my luggage. I simply brought it for her. As I expected, she never used it. She packed it away in her kitchen cabinet. It was too precious. Not for everyday use.

I bought her a dishwasher too, though by then I knew she would probably never use it. After years of disuse, the engine stalled.

Did I believe these things I bought would make up for words locked in my heart that couldn't leave my lips?

I think it gave my mother a sense of security to know

that if important people dropped by, she would be ready to entertain them with her good china and her expensive silverware. She would only have to open the doors of her cabinet and pull out the drawers of her credenza. Shouldn't it have given me a sense of security too to know I could depend on her if and when I needed her? Words should not have been necessary. For either of us.

I get to the business of drafting words. I write what I believe to be true. My mother was the best wife she could be, she was the best mother she could be. Her heart was her china cabinet, it was her credenza, where she stored her love for us. More times than I can count she had unlocked that heart whenever we needed her.

26

At the church the next morning, our father refuses to get out of the limousine. The hearse waits. My sisters try to persuade him to come with us inside the church; my brothers try. Our father will not budge. He has curled himself into a tight ball against the plush leather seat in the back of the limousine. His jaw is set, his eyes fixed in a blank stare directed outside the window. The organ music rises and flows out of the church. The pallbearers walk past us, peer inside the limousine, and turn away, shaking their heads in sympathy.

"Come, Daddy," I say, and tug his arm gently. His arm is rigid as steel.

One brother leaves the limousine and reports back to us: "Every pew in the church is taken. People are crushed against each other in their seats. The aisles on both sides are four people deep and stretch from the top line of pews to the bottom."

Hundreds have come to pay their respects to our mother, from Trinidad's high society to the person in the street. The prime minister is there with his entourage, so too is a group of villagers who are weeping silently.

By now a crowd has gathered on the steps and on the pavement outside the church. Soon there are murmurings. *What's holding things up? What's wrong? Somebody sick?*

My father is not sick. If he wants to, he can move his legs. If he wants to, he can get out of the car. He is not confused either. He is acutely aware of where he is. This is the church where he and his wife have gone to Mass every Sunday for more than a quarter of a century. He was here with her just days ago.

"We won't leave your side," my sisters promise. "We'll stay close to you." Our father remains rigid. They plead with him. "We can't start without you, Daddy."

He still does not respond. His stare gets more fixed, more determined, his limbs more unyielding.

Time passes. Ten minutes. More. The funeral director comes to the car door. "Can I help? Can I get a wheelchair?"

My father looks up. His thin lips clamp together into a straight line above his rigid jaw. We know that look. It's been years—we were young, still children—but we have not forgotten. When our father said no, he meant no. Nothing changed his mind. He was set on his course, as clearly as he is now. It would be futile to try again. We direct the pallbearers to begin. We follow our mother's coffin into the church. Richard stays with our father in the limousine; he keeps the doors open.

After the eulogy, the Eucharist. The priest comes down the steps of the altar and stands before the Communion rails. The congregation waits for us. We are expected to receive Communion before they do. I look around me. My siblings are still on their knees. With one exception our first marriages have ended in divorce, or in years of separation, or we have married someone who was divorced. All sins in the Catholic Church. For those who remarried, or those who during their long separation had sexual relationships with someone other than their spouse, the sin of adultery. Jacqueline turns to face us, a question in her eyes. But she is free to receive Communion; her first marriage was annulled. Then David stands up, no hesitation in his movement. David is divorced and has remarried a divorcée. "Come," he says. We all stand up. My brother starts the line and we follow him. We honor our mother. We are her children.

After he has given us the Eucharist, the priest walks down the middle aisle of the church. The hushed whisperings begin. *Where is he going?* Heads turn. The priest walks through the open doors of the church to the yard outside. For five long minutes, in the middle of a Mass, we are left without a priest.

Richard tells me that when the priest stepped into the limousine, my father sat up and opened his mouth. The priest placed the Eucharist on his tongue. My father sat back down again, but something in him had changed. His limbs had loosened, the muscles in his face had relaxed.

27

At the cemetery, my father is vibrantly alert, full of life. He takes charge. "Watch those gravediggers," he instructs us.

In Trinidad, as in most of the Caribbean, the grave is dug in the presence of family and friends. While the gravediggers work, we sing our mother's favorite hymns. Jacqueline's friend, who has a beautiful voice, sings the Ave Maria. I have a favorite hymn too. Not long ago I had sung it for my parents. I was sitting on their bed, next to my mother who was propped up on her pillow. My father was on his bedside armchair grumbling about the folly of death. It did not make sense to him that life should end, he said. I sang the hymn that consoles me:

Be not afraid, I go before you always,
Come, follow me and I will give you rest . . .

My mother was pleased. "Hear that, Waldo. There's nothing to fear. God has more plans for you."

Now we all sing the hymn. *Be not afraid*. The dirt piles higher on either side of the hole the gravediggers have made. Eventually all we see are the tops of the gravediggers' heads. My father comes to the edge of the grave. "Make sure you go down nine feet," he instructs the men, then turns to me. "Tell them nine feet."

Six feet for one person, nine if another is to be put in the same grave.

28

My novel *Anna In-Between* is published the following year. My mother had read most of my other novels in manuscript but not this one. She died before her cataracts could be removed and so she never had a chance to read it in any form. But I had told her about the book. I said to her I had written a novel about a character that was somewhat based on her. She gave me that enigmatic smile that always left me feeling uncomfortably like a child again, though I was already a grandmother of two. It was as if she were holding all the cards and I, put at a distinct disadvantage, had already lost before the game was played. "Go ahead," she said.

"You won't mind?"

"I always love your novels. Write what you want to. I won't mind, no matter what you say."

Was she giving me permission? Did she already know what I had written? Or was it that she believed I would never cast her in a light she would not approve? That I would be fair to her?

Some of my most ardent supporters tell me that though they love the novel, they think I am too hard on Beatrice Sinclair, Anna's mother. They want to like her but they find it hard to sympathize with a woman who withholds hugs and kisses from her child.

Anna thinks so too and she tries to be forgiving of her mother's seeming emotional detachment from her. She recites an old man's prayer:

Change ah we heart, O Lord. Change ah we heart.
Change ah we heart like mongoose kinna change he skin
under rock bottom.

My friend Pat Ramdeen is more sympathetic. She says Beatrice Sinclair pushes her daughter because she wants her to succeed. She wants to toughen her for a world that is not always kind to women. She wants her to be independent, self-reliant. She cannot afford to coddle Anna.

Pat, like me, is an immigrant from Trinidad. We both had to bear in silence the shock of being plunged suddenly into frigid weather after the warmth of our tropical sun. We both had to endure the searing loneliness of being in a strange land among strange people. We know firsthand the heart-tugging longing for family and friends. We were scholarship girls, beholden to the generosity of the Marian nuns and their devoted donors. We could not be ungrateful. So we exercised restraint. Every hour of every day, of every month, of every year for four years, restraint kept us from falling apart.

"The immigrant survives by forgetting," says the narrator of *Anna In-Between* as Anna tries to persuade herself not think of her grassy green tropical island, redolent with the fragrance of brightly colored flowering trees. "The immigrant erases from her consciousness the past that is too painful for her to bear."

It takes another novel for Anna to come to the realization that there are two sides to restraint. By the end of *Boundaries*, the novel that follows *Anna In-Between*, she has an epiphany: "It occurs to Anna now that restraint can protect even though it excludes. She has the answer to her question: her mother is restrained but perhaps because she wants to protect her."

The epiphany is mine. I place it in Anna's mouth. It comes to me in that miraculous year, when by some strange collision of events I am in Trinidad three times, the last time a month before my mother dies.

So are both novels, *Anna In-Between* and *Boundaries*, about me and my family? I think to some extent all novels are camouflaged autobiography. The facts may be inaccurate, even false, but the emotions and ideas resonate from the writer's experience, something he or she feels passionate about, ideas the writer is anxious to explore.

Richard, who has read both of these novels, interrogates me. I don't believe such and such happened, he tells me. I explain that both books are works of fiction, not autobiography or memoir. I may have been inspired by the facts, but I took the liberty to make use of them as they suited the stories thematically and artistically. Yes, the books' base about a mother who has breast cancer, who discovers—no, admits—she has a tumor as large as an orange in her left breast, and another one as large as a lemon under her arm, is very much our mother's story, but it was just the blueprint for the novels I wrote. I know no Dr. Lee Pak, nor Dr. Ramdoolal, nor Paula, nor Paul Bishop; they are all invented characters.

"Though . . ." I pause for the effect I want; he is curious about my personal life after D—.

"Though what?" he asks, wide-eyed, caught on my hook.

"Though it would be nice to have a Paul Bishop in my life."

"And why don't you? Why *didn't* you?"

"It's all about timing," I say. "My Paul Bishop always arrived at the wrong time, either I was not free or he was not free. Then when we were both free, we were too set in our ways to make compromises. Anyhow, I'm not Anna. I would still be seething with resentment if what had happened to her at work had happened to me. Anna concedes too quickly; Paul encourages her to concede too quickly. I would need a more supportive Paul Bishop."

It takes my brother a moment to respond, and when he does, he looks away from me. "You are as ambitious as Anna," he mutters.

I don't think Richard says this spitefully, but I know he doesn't mean it as a compliment either. Men of my generation are generally wary of ambitious women.

"Anna, you will note, is the only child of John and Beatrice Sinclair," I say, refusing to go down the path I sense he wants to lead me with gripes about his own relationships. "We are eleven. More importantly, the plot in the first novel turns on Beatrice's refusal to have surgery in the US, which would never have been true for our mother. She was a patriot, but she believed in the superiority of medicine in America." I go on, but he stops me midsentence.

"And what about John Sinclair's infidelity?"

Ahh, he has me there! How do I reconcile my father's undying love for my mother with the extramarital affairs I believe he had through many of their years together?

One of my mother's favorite novels was Gabriel García Márquez's *Love in the Time of Cholera*. She loved it so much, she read it twice. In that novel, Florentino Ariza professes his "eternal fidelity and everlasting love" for Fermina Daza, which he claims was never broken in the fifty-one years, nine months, and four days since they parted. Yet the reader knows that during those fifty-one years, nine months, and four days, Florentino Ariza had many sexual trysts and some enduring love affairs. Still, in Florentino Ariza's mind he has remained a virgin for Fermina Daza, his one true love.

My father, too, denied he had ever been unfaithful to my mother, though there were nights I lived through loud arguments and tears as my mother accused him of having lovers. Of course, we knew she was right, but my father would become incensed if any of us made the slightest suggestion that he had been unfaithful to her. Always he swore he loved her. He did not lie—he never lied—not by commission at least, though I would have to say he lied by omission, sidestepping our questions, never acknowledging our accusations, always claiming that our mother was the only woman who mattered in his life.

In his last years with my mother, he was more direct. "Affairs? I don't know what you're talking about." He would say this with such conviction that we would find ourselves questioning the accuracy of our long-held beliefs. Did we have proof? Had any of us seen our father in a compromising position with another woman? Could we name names?

Gabriel García Márquez claims that "what matters in life is not what happens to you but what you remember and how you remember it." My father remembers that he adored my mother. His mind does not allow him to remember that he was unfaithful to her. My mother seemed to share the same recollections. On the last two days I spent with her and my father, we talked about their lives. "I was lucky," my mother said. "I don't know why God was so good to me. I have a loving husband and all my eleven children are alive and well and successful."

Indeed it was amazing. Both my parents had lived to their nineties and not one of their eleven children has suffered a serious illness. We are all alive. They did not have to bear the single most painful tragedy a parent can experience: the death of a child.

"I had a good life," I heard my father say to my mother one day. "I was lucky. The woman I loved married me."

And my mother answered: "You were always a good husband to me."

POSTSCRIPT

My father died seven months after my mother. As he wished, he was buried in the same grave with her. Without his wife, my father seemed to find little reason for living. She had given him the security and stability he'd yearned for all his life as the darkest of his parents' children, a brilliant man whose rise up the ranks of the British colonial system, and, later, the British- and Dutch-owned Shell Oil Company, was always threatened in a society that placed inordinate value on skin color.

During those seven months after my mother's death, my sister Mary went often to Trinidad to be with our father. She tells me that the entwined mango trees, under which shade he often sat, continued to bear fruit, though the only fruit she remembers it bearing were the small, sweet starch mangoes my mother loved. Since my father died, Mary has returned to Trinidad three more times, once during the mango season. Never has she seen a single mango on those entwined trees. As far as I know, never have they borne fruit again.